DIMENSIONS OF URBAN SOCIAL STRUCTURE

The physical segregation of social groups in industrial cities has long attracted the attention of social scientist and casual observer alike. In Australia the possibility of mapping the social ecology of large cities has been limited by the absence of sufficiently detailed census information, a gap remedied in 1961 by the provision of a new range of small area data.

Here the author exploits the existence of the new information to present the first intensive social anatomy of any Australian metropolis. Statistics on the residential concentration and segregation of seventy socioeconomic, demographic, ethnic, and religious categories are examined, and the vast complexity and range of these data are reduced by sophisticated techniques of statistical analysis to three theoretically meaningful constructs—social rank, familism, and ethnicity. These constructs are used to develop a typology of social areas which serves as the basis for developing an understanding of, and further hypotheses about, urban social structure.

Not only does this analysis present a self-contained study of Australia's second largest metropolis, but detailed maps and statistical appendixes provide a benchmark for future social investigations into the urban scene—on subjects such as political preference, immigrant adjustment, poverty, crime, delinquency, and urban planning.

DR F. LANCASTER JONES is a graduate of the University of Sydney and of the Australian National University. He has published widely on various aspects of Australian sociology. Among his interests are the demography of the Australian Aborigines and the absorption of Italian immigrants in Australia, the last of which won him a knighthood from the Italian Government in 1967. He is at present a Fellow in Sociology in the Research School of Social Sciences at the Australian National University.

*A Demographic Survey of the Aboriginal Population of
the Northern Territory, with Special Reference to
Bathurst Island Mission*, 1963

F. LANCASTER JONES

Dimensions of Urban Social Structure

The Social Areas of
Melbourne, Australia

UNIVERSITY OF TORONTO PRESS

First published in Canada, the United States, Great Britain,
and Europe by University of Toronto Press

Reprined in paperback 2017
ISBN 978-0-8020-1662-1 (cloth)
ISBN 978-1-4875-9214-1 (paper)

Cover designed by John Pitson

Preface

The basic purpose of this monograph is to contribute to our understanding of the structure of Australian metropolises—the social environment in which two-thirds of Australians live—through the detailed analysis of census data about the social characteristics of the people who live in them. The work is based almost entirely on a single set of data—from the 1961 census—and pertains to a single city—Melbourne, the capital of the State of Victoria. It is the first such study to be published for any Australian city—apart from my less extensive pilot study of Canberra—but I hope that future studies will build on this foundation, to produce in time a systematic, cumulative, and comparative body of knowledge about the social structure of Australian cities.

To some, no doubt, this study may seem to document the obvious. But for others—I hope the majority—it will raise questions about the nature of Australian society that hitherto may have been played down or even ignored. I am not myself particularly impressed by the familiar cry of 'stating the obvious', since *any* statement about social life is bound to be obvious to *someone*. After all, the information with which the sociologist has to deal is public property: it is made in the minds of men. If his systematic analysis of social life produces so-called 'commonsense' results, we can have no complaint. Surprise may be the essence of mystery stories and science fiction but it is not the test of fruitful and important sociological research. Indeed, I do not know how one could surprise the common sense that affirms on the one hand that 'Too many cooks spoil the broth', but on the other that 'Many hands make light work'; that advises 'Penny wise, pound foolish', yet warns 'Look after the pennies and the pounds will look after themselves'. Common sense in fact is little more than a treasure-trove of mutually contradictory statements in terms of which *any* social event or human experience can find a reassuring interpretation. While I would never presume to steal a march upon common sense, it is obviously worthwhile to investigate the conditions under which one segment of common sense may be more applicable than another. Of course the complaint that the results of a sociological study are self-evident is often no more than an ill-disguised technique for distracting attention from facts which, while obvious, are more conveniently ignored. But this is an issue that I can leave to my readers to judge.

In a statistical study of social life an author runs many risks. One, of course, is that of boring his readers. To those who have a distaste for statistical presentation I can only say that I have done my best to soften the blows. I can assure them that they have been spared much of the quantitative information that went to provide the basis of this study. A second difficulty perhaps is that of overcoming a possible feeling among some readers that many aspects of social life cannot easily be reduced to numbers. I have some sympathy for that feeling, and indeed initially I had hoped to extend the findings of this present study with other, more qualitative types of information. But in the end—mainly because of insufficient time and the pressure of other research—that proved to be impossible.

Yet I should not be too defensive about offering what is largely a quantitative analysis of urban social structure. Qualitative studies, however informative, are sometimes ignored as impressionistic, and very often we only begin to confront a situation when its limits have been set out in unmistakable quantitative terms. Moreover, the idea that human action is ultimately irreducible to numbers and quantities is frequently a sentimental refuge, a defence against too close a scrutiny of the foundations of social life. Yet in complex and highly interdependent societies such as our own, the bases of social organisation must be closely scrutinised. Society, after all, is only a human construction representing the collective experience of successive generations. If it is to serve the ends that we set it, we must understand and fashion it as well as we can.

Perhaps a specific word of explanation is required about the units of analysis used in this study. They are very small localities within Melbourne (groups of census collectors' districts). Because they have no names they can be identified only by reference to code numbers and a base map. The difficulties in obtaining a suitable base map for this study were considerable, but I hope that my efforts to communicate the results of my analysis to the reader have been successful. A well-known set of small localities would, of course, have been of great value if available. As it is, I have provided detailed keys to the various maps that appear in the monograph, and in appendixes I have related these units of analysis to the only sets of named localities in relatively wide usage—local government areas and postal districts. The following abbreviations are used in different parts of the text: ACD, aggregated collectors' districts; CBD, central business district; CD, census collector's district.

In writing this monograph I have relied upon the help of many people and institutions. I cannot name them all, but they include the Commonwealth Bureau of Census and Statistics for supplying published and unpublished census data; the Melbourne and Metropolitan Board of Works for supplying base maps; Miss Mary Rose, Mr Trevor Letty, Mr Peter Tindale, Mr Jack Palmer, Dr Bill Williams, and Mr Peter Milne for computer programming assistance; Mrs Bridget Boucher, Miss Margo Huxley, and Mrs Sam Mueller for research assistance at various stages in the project; Dr J. Zubrzycki, Dr J. J. Mol, Dr Robert Brown, and other colleagues and graduate students in the Research School of Social Sciences at the Australian National University for comments on sections of the draft; Professor Jean Martin, Professor Leonard Broom, and Professor Ronald Taft for comments on the final manuscript; and Mrs Betty Gamble and Miss Ann Godfery, who typed and retyped the text and tables. I deeply appreciate their assistance and, where necessary, their criticism. The final responsibility for what follows is, of course, my own.

F.L.J.

Contents

Tables

Figures

1

Introduction

Throughout the world the number of people who live in towns is constantly increasing. In both advanced and developing countries the growth of cities exceeds the growth of population. In some of these countries the concentration of population into a few relatively densely settled localities is a new phenomenon. But in Australia it has, if anything, been the traditional mode of settlement. Australia today ranks among the most highly urbanised countries of the world, and in terms of population concentration is perhaps the most urbanised country in the world. As the most recent (1966) census showed, 58 per cent of Australia's total population lived in seven metropolitan cities.

In spite of the fact that to most Australians towns and cities have been a traditional social environment, few studies of the social structure of Australian cities exist. One can point to Oeser and Hammond's early study in Melbourne, to some works on rural townships in different parts of Australia, and to a number of specialist papers dealing with limited aspects of the urban scene (Oeser and Hammond 1954; Connell *et al.* 1957; Oeser and Emery 1954; Campbell 1963; Zubrzycki 1964; K. W. Robinson 1962; Brennan 1963; Scott 1965; Johnston 1966). But beyond these there are no studies which deal systematically or extensively with the general social structure of any Australian metropolis.

To some extent this relative lack of urban sociological studies reflects the late development of sociology as an academic discipline in this country. Even now sociology is taught in only about one in three universities in Australia. To a lesser degree it reflects the unavailability until recently of certain types of social statistics which might encourage detailed analyses of urban social structure, similar to those that have long existed for many cities in the United States and elsewhere. But there are, happily, clear indications that both these limitations are becoming less serious, and that the social structure of urban Australia, largely *terra incognita*, is slowly being mapped.

Although, as the title indicates, the present work is concerned with dimensions of urban social structure, I should emphasise immediately that its coverage is less comprehensive than this title might at first suggest. To begin with, my analysis relies almost exclusively on a single source of data (the Australian census) for a single city (Melbourne) at one point in time (1961). Moreover, most of the detailed analysis presented in this study does not relate directly to individuals, but to collections of individuals—the resident populations of census collectors' districts, which are the basic units of enumeration used in Australian censuses. Data on individuals as such are, of course, introduced at various points in the analysis, but mainly to illustrate or clarify the discussion of information on residential areas. To put it briefly, the present study sets out to identify dimensions of urban social structure through an analysis of the social characteristics of the numerous residential areas which go to make up the shape of a city, which reflect and in part determine the social networks of its population. Since what follows rests so heavily on such data, it is obviously essential to amplify these introductory remarks by specifying what types of analyses these residential data do, and do not, permit.

Residential areas and urban social structure

It is a matter of casual as well as sociological observation that the population of large cities is not randomly distributed. In fact so pervasive are the factors affecting the location of residential and other land uses in modern industrial cities that given a few general geographical and historical facts a trained observer could readily predict the location of skid row, the bright lights district, nob hill, areas of minority concentration, and the like in such cities. Indeed Ernest Burgess, the proponent of one of the most persuasive theories of urban growth, conceived the social and spatial structure of modern cities in terms of a series of concentric zones around the central business district —a conceptualisation which has been shown to be of very wide utility in spite of (perhaps because of) its high level of generality (Burgess 1925).

This view of the city as a complex network of localised social groups —a mosaic of social worlds, to use Louis Wirth's phrase (1938)—has received its most extensive and impressive documentation in what became known as the Chicago school of human ecology, dating from the 1920s with the now classic writings of men like Robert Park, Ernest Burgess, Roderick McKenzie, Louis Wirth, and their numerous colleagues and students. The impact of this school on the course of urban sociology in the United States has been documented in many places, and while the approach of urban ecologists has been modified and diversified over the years, the Chicago school remains a dominant influence in this field of study today.

An early concern of urban ecologists was with the typical spatial arrangements of population that industrial cities everywhere display. This concern can perhaps be best illustrated with a quotation from an influential paper by Robert Park, entitled 'The Urban Community as a Spatial Pattern and a Moral Order' (in Burgess 1926:11-12) :

> Every typical urban area is likely to contain a characteristic selection of the population of the community as a whole. In great cities the divergence in manners, in standards of living, and in general outlook on life in different urban areas is often astonishing. The difference in sex and age groups, perhaps the most significant indexes of social life, are strikingly divergent for different natural areas. There are regions in the city where there are almost no children, areas occupied by the residential hotels, for example. There are regions occupied where the number of children is relatively high: in the slums, in the middle-class residential suburbs, to which the newly married usually graduate from their first honeymoon apartments in the city. There are other areas occupied almost wholly by young unmarried people, boy and girl bachelors. There are regions where people almost never vote, except at national elections; regions where the divorce rate is higher than it is for any state in the Union, and other regions in the same city where there are almost no divorces. There are areas infested by boy gangs and the athletic and political clubs into which the members of these gangs or the gangs themselves frequently graduate. There are regions in which the suicide rate is excessive; regions in which there is, as recorded by statistics, an excessive amount of juvenile delinquency, and other regions in which there is almost none.
>
> All this emphasizes the importance of location, position, and mobility as indexes for measuring, describing, and eventually explaining, social phenomena.

In their studies of the structure of cities the ecologists borrowed freely from the concepts and terminology of animal and plant ecology. While this is not the place to attempt a full discussion of the validity or utility of these concepts as applied in the sociological analysis of urban communities, one concept—that of the natural area—is of fundamental importance in the present context and requires detailed comment.

An early definition saw the natural area as a 'geographical area characterised both by a physical individuality and by the cultural characteristics of the people who live in it' (Zorbaugh 1926:223). That is to say a natural area can be identified as a specific geographical location within the city and in terms of the distinctive cultural forms and distinguishing social relationships displayed by its resident population. Such areas, designated by such colourful titles as Hobohemia, Little

Italy, the Ghetto, Skid Row, Towertown, the Gold Coast and so on, were called natural areas because in the view of the ecologists they arose, not out of conscious planning, but out of tendencies inherent in the nature of urban life itself. They could be viewed in a sense as the natural habitat of distinct social groups (for example an immigrant ghetto, an upper class preserve, or a family-oriented dormitory suburb), just as in the world of nature we might identify the forests, plains, deserts, and mountains as the natural habitat of different plant and animal species. The natural areas into which the urban community typically resolved itself were seen as the result of a sifting and sorting process (competition) leading to the physical segregation of different social and cultural types. This working hypothesis, as Park termed it, seemed to be justified both by general reasoning about the nature of social relationships in large, culturally heterogeneous cities and by actual observation of urban life itself. The detailed researches of the Chicago school bear impressive testimony to the impact of such ideas.

How, then, was one to identify the natural areas of a city? In operational terms, natural areas were identified by the ecologists either through participant observation and community study methods, or by analysis of detailed information on the social characteristics of small residential areas, typically census tracts or aggregations of them. The idea of census tracts was originated by Dr Walter Laidlaw in 1906 as a means of analysing changes in the structure of American cities in a more meaningful way than was possible with arbitrarily defined local government and administrative statistical divisions. For the 1910 census, tracts were established in eight cities, although at the time New York City was the only city that utilised these census tract statistics. By the time of the most recent American census in 1960, the number of tracted areas had increased to 180, and information was available for 23,123 census tracts, comprising about half the population of the United States. Although originally census tracts were designed to be of roughly equal acreage, a fundamental principle underlying the concept of the census tract was that these areas should contain as homogeneous a population as possible. The social characteristics usually adopted in assessing homogeneity were economic, but racial, ethnic, and demographic characteristics were also ranked as important (Hauser 1956; U.S. Bureau of the Census 1961; Schmid 1938).

Although, as I have tried to suggest, the idea of 'natural areas' and the division of cities into census tracts were closely interrelated, in practice as well as in theory many problems arose. On the practical side there were difficulties in defining the tracts. Should tracts be kept uniform in area or population, and what criteria should be adopted in determining the homogeneity of the resident population? Should tracts conform to administrative boundaries, or should they define uniquely in geographical space the physical limits of a social group? Even when such questions had been satisfactorily answered for one point in time, there was the further intransigent problem that processes of social change and population redistribution would inevitably alter the social characteristics of many tracts so greatly that they would become inappropriate units of analysis in terms of their original definition. At the theoretical level there were substantial problems in specifying the concept of 'homogeneity'—still a difficult concept—and in deciding whether natural areas were 'real', or simply a construct employed by researchers to understand the structure of the urban community. How significant, in any case, could common residence in a single neighbourhood be assumed to be in determining the behaviour of urbanites?

To the early ecologists, natural areas were real geographical and cultural units. The main task was simply to identify them and study their composition and relationship to the total city. Natural areas were, like everything else in the social domain, subject to change, but social change could be studied in terms of the basic ecological processes of competition, segregation, invasion, and succession. Before long, however, these views came to be challenged. Empirical studies of the social composition of census tracts indicated that the assumption of homogeneity was subject to substantial qualification for many residential districts, and doubt was expressed as to whether natural areas could be said to exist at all under the conditions specified by traditional ecology. In an important case study Hatt (1946) demonstrated that in the central district of Seattle the location and number of natural areas varied arbitrarily according to the criterion employed; they varied, too, when the size of the initial unit of analysis was varied (for example small city blocks compared with larger census tracts). He concluded that the larger unit gave an unrealistic impression of homogeneity and further showed that the spatial distributions of different ethnic groups overlapped considerably. Yet the social characteristics of these ethnic minorities differed markedly one from the other, and from those of other residents in the same area. Important as these findings were, Hatt did not interpret his results as an outright rejection of the concept of the natural area, but rather as a warning against certain prevalent and largely untested assumptions:

> If ecological phenomena are viewed as a frame of reference, and the concept of natural area as a construct within that frame, then the data presented in this paper could be assigned to natural areas.

B

The location of the areas would depend entirely on the problem defined by the student. The fact that these areas might overlap would be a matter of no great consequence since the utility of these areas would be determined by the point of view of the investigator and the problem at hand. However, if the concept of natural area is reified, and these areas sought as actual entities, then their very existence is in doubt, if the data presented in this paper are at all representative of urban patterns (Hatt 1946:427).

Recent research into the pattern of population distribution within urban areas has largely conformed to Hatt's view. Researchers have grown more cautious in their interpretation of aggregate residential data, and although in many respects current research interests in urban spatial structure have much in common with the studies by earlier ecologists, the limitations of census tract data as a means of studying the social organisation of cities are widely appreciated. There has also been some movement away from an interest in spatial patterns as such, towards a concern with the ways in which social structure is reflected in geographical space, a trend illustrated by social area analysis (Shevky and Williams 1949).

Social area analysis is a method of urban analysis which emerged in 1949 from the University of California at Los Angeles. It was noteworthy for its independence from the Chicago tradition in urban sociology, for its attempt to view the spatial segregation of social groups against the broad canvas of social change in modern industrial societies, and for the instant controversy it aroused and still arouses. In criticising the lack of comparative emphasis in classical ecology, Shevky and Williams (1949:1) dismissed the Chicago school in one short paragraph:

> It is partly as a consequence of this [startling lack of comparative knowledge] that the brilliant formulations of Robert Park, which provided the original impetus for the detailed ecological studies of Chicago, ultimately resulted in the development of a non-experimental, descriptive method. The influence of this tradition in the study of the city still persists in research and teaching, but its organizing principles no longer appear congruent with the postulates and theories with which social scientists at present operate.

They then proceeded without further reference, or indeed apparent debt, to the Chicago school in developing their own method of urban analysis, in which they interpreted the residential differentiation of social groups in industrial cities in terms of three constructs—social rank, urbanisation, and segregation—which they derived from a consideration of master trends in the total society.

As I have already indicated, social area analysis was received with less than enthusiasm in some quarters. In 1955 a second volume was published, one major aim of which was to restate the basic orientation of this approach and to specify the steps in construct formation and index construction involved in this new method of urban analysis. Since the publication of that second monograph (Shevky and Bell 1955) a number of research papers relating to social area analysis have appeared, some favourable, some unfavourable, and some equivocal in their evaluation of the method. At the same time the intellectual debate concerning this controversial issue has thickened appreciably, and social area analysis has been accused of being unsound in its theoretical derivation, of employing constructs with little empirical meaning, and of introducing a complicated series of statistical operations without any congruent gain in interpretative meaning (Hawley and Duncan 1957; Arsdol *et al.* 1961, 1962). These attacks have been met by vigorous defence, with little sign as yet of a final resolution of the central issues.

Despite this substantial area of controversy, the present study draws heavily from the work of social area analysts, particularly from their general view that the residential patterning of social groups can be largely understood in terms of three factors—social rank, urbanisation, and segregation. The next chapter deals more fully, and hopefully more adequately, with some of the more important criticisms that have been levelled at social area analysis, partly because the structure of the present analysis owes much to the work of Shevky and his associates and partly as a vehicle for presenting the general principles underlying this particular study of Melbourne. The main task is to identify factors affecting the social differentiation and stratification of urban populations and to examine the processes by which socially differentiated population groups come also to be residentially segregated, if indeed that proves to be the case. But first some more general comments need to be made.

To persons unfamiliar with the history of research into the social characteristics of residential areas, it may not be altogether clear why sociologists trouble to analyse information on census tracts or collectors' districts. After all, they are no longer regarded as natural areas in the sense that their residents uniformly constitute a meaningful social group with distinctive ways of behaving. Nor is it permissible to argue that what is true for the population of the area as a whole is necessarily true for any given resident, since this would require a level of homogeneity in social attributes that needs to be demonstrated rather than assumed. Granted that this is the case, why bother at all to analyse and systematise the vast array of information relating

to such areas? To answer this question we must first confront the logical problem of the relationship between information for an individual
person and information for an aggregate of individuals—to adopt the
terminology of Patricia Kendall and Paul Lazarsfeld (1955), the relationship between a personal datum and a unit datum.

As Kendall and Lazarsfeld convincingly demonstrate, personal data
and unit data are not logically interchangeable, although in certain cases
the use of unit data will lead to a conclusion that individual data also
support (W. J. Robinson 1950; Menzel 1950). A concrete example may
help to explain the problem. In the present study it was found that areas
with a high proportion of unemployed men also had a high proportion
of immigrants. There are two possible explanations of this observation:
that immigrants are more often unemployed than the native-born (a
hypothesis that can be tested directly only with individual data cross-
tabulating occupational status by birthplace); or that the unemployed
live in the poorest section of the city, which is also where immigrants
live (an ecological, not an individual, relationship). In the first case
individual data would support the conclusion from ecological data; in
the second case they need not do so, since even if the immigrants were
not unemployed in greater proportions than the native-born, the same
unit or ecological correlation would be observed. It is critical to distinguish these two cases and to avoid the ecological fallacy of inferring
an individual correlation solely from an ecological one. However,
while the question of the interchangeability of individual and unit
data has been important in the development of ecological studies,
there is another use of unit data which is properly independent of this
issue. To quote Kendall and Lazarsfeld (1955:296),

> There is no reason why unit data cannot be used to characterize
> individuals in the unit. A man who does not have malaria in a
> [combat] unit where the incidence of malaria is very low probably
> feels differently about his state of health than does the man who
> has no malaria but serves in a unit with high incidence and there-
> fore is surrounded by malaria cases . . .
> In terms of actual analysis the matter can be restated in the fol-
> lowing terms: just as we can classify people by demographic vari-
> ables or by their attitudes, we can also classify them by the kind of
> environment in which they live. The appropriate variables for such
> a classification are likely to be unit data. A survey analysis would
> then cover both personal and unit data simultaneously.

This illustrates the reasoning that will be applied in the present
study. It will be argued that the dwelling area represents a salient
environment within which many important social relationships occur
and that knowledge about that environment provides an important

key to understanding social behaviour. Moreover, each area in the city tends to acquire a social evaluation reflecting the social characteristics of its inhabitants, and residential areas become in time socially import- ant symbols. As well, each has a specific location with respect to the major urban facilities of employment, recreation, and transportation, and contains more or less permanent characteristics (such as topo- graphy and buildings) which are differentially evaluated by members of the urban community. All these characteristics serve as a basis for classifying residential areas. By classifying areas according to such criteria we can make statements about the relative dispersal, concen- tration, or segregation of various social categories throughout the urban community as well as make predictions about individual be- haviour in different types of area—predictions that can be tested against appropriate individual data. Social area analysts have extended their research in precisely this way (Bell 1965:235-64).

By formulating the problem in this way and concentrating attention on the social characteristics of residential areas as such, initial assump- tions about homogeneity are unnecessary. If an area is largely homo- geneous, this will be reflected in our analysis; if it is heterogeneous, this will also emerge. More than this, differences between areas raise important sets of further questions concerning the behaviour, attitudes, and expectations of persons whose characteristics deviate markedly from those of other residents in the same area. In what ways, for ex- ample, do families with high socioeconomic status living in predomin- antly low status areas differ from similar families living in largely high status areas? What characterises immigrants who live, not in the ethnic enclaves of a city, but in areas with few other immigrants? Is neighbourhood an important determinant of social relationships among urbanites, or can systematic differences be established among different types of areas? These and other questions emerge as lines of future investigations from studies of the social composition of residen- tial areas. Perhaps none of these interests is adequately reflected in the material under analysis, but this should be seen as the result of short- ages of time and relevant information, rather than as deficiencies in approach and method.

Sources

As already indicated, this monograph is mainly concerned with aggre- gate data for small residential areas of Melbourne, census collectors' districts (CDs). The 1961 census was the first Australian census to pro- vide a wide range of such information. CDs are the basic geographical unit of enumeration in Australian censuses and are designed to be small enough to be handled by one census collector in a period of ten days. Since Australian censuses are conducted by self-enumeration, the task of the census collector is to distribute census forms prior to census night and to recover completed forms after census night. The major consideration in designing a network of CDs is this workload, the only other constraint being that CD boundaries have to conform to those of local government areas and statistical divisions. In most areas, of course, attention is given to choosing clear boundaries in delimiting CDs, and streets and natural features are commonly adopted as boundary lines. Social homogeneity, however, is not a criterion in the delimitation of CDs (Linge 1965:65).

The current framework of CD divisions in Melbourne was established for use in the 1947 census. Comparability since that time has been maintained, except where population growth and changes in local government area boundaries have necessitated subdivision of existing CDs. In 1961 the Melbourne metropolitan area comprised 2,107 occupied CDs, with an average population of 907 persons. However, because of differences in density and changes in population distribution since 1947, considerable variation exists in the population size of CDs. In 1961 the size distribution of CDs was as follows:

Population Size	Per cent
Less than 500	10
500-749	22
750-999	31
1,000-1,249	23
1,250-1,499	10
1,500 and over	4
Total	100

More important than variation as such is the fact that differences in CD size tend to be systematically related to other factors. Over time CDs located near the centre of the city tend to have smaller populations because of deteriorating housing conditions and the conversion of residential land to non-residential purposes, whereas those towards the periphery of the city grow larger because of population growth. For example, in the central City of Melbourne average CD size had declined by 1961 to only 680 persons, compared with 1,200 persons in Box Hill Municipality, a rapidly growing area nine miles east of the city centre. Since one of the methods of analysis employed in this study involved the calculation of ecological correlations, in which each CD receives an equal weight, it seemed unreasonable to accept systematic variations in size that would effectively over-represent areas of declining population. This difficulty might have been partially countered by the use of some type of weighting system, but this would have left untouched the important but often neglected problem of the meaningfulness of rates based on small populations (Ross 1933; Chaddock 1934). This issue would have been acute in the present study, where one-third of the CDs contained fewer than 750 persons.

To overcome this difficulty without resorting to extremely coarse categories of social characteristics, a new series of aggregated collectors' districts (ACDs) was constructed. It was anticipated that this new series would serve to limit the range of variability in population size, to randomise any residual variation, and to improve the reliability of some measures by increasing the base from which they were calculated. An optimum size of approximately 3,000 persons was settled upon for the new series, since this would effectively reduce the number of units for analysis to around 700 but still provide very detailed information on the residential differentiation of social groups. It is worth pointing out that geographical units of even this size are still smaller than most census tracts in American cities.

One further advantage of this aggregation was that it allowed some scope for testing the similarity of CDs grouped together. I could, of course, have explored this whole question in much greater detail, but with over two thousand CDs this would have been a major project in itself. Prior to aggregation the central business district and CDs with primarily institutional or non-private accommodation (indicated by an average of six persons or more per occupied dwelling) were excluded. For the remaining 2,042 CDs profiles were constructed showing the percentage of private houses, the percentage of owner-occupied houses, and the percentage of private houses built since the preceding census in 1954. An initial aggregation of CDs to an optimum size of approximately 3,000 persons was then made, the only controls being that areas so aggregated were contiguous and in the same local government area. The profiles of the constituent CDs in each new group were then compared and where possible dissimilar CDs were regrouped. As a crude measure of dissimilarity the semi-interquartile ranges of the three measures in the profile were used, giving a range of tolerance of 12·5, 20·0, and 10·0 per cent respectively.

A detailed analysis of the internal variation among these measures has been made. In 55 per cent of the ACDs the range of variation in the percentage of private houses among the original CDs was less than 10 per cent. For owner-occupancy and period of building, 59 and 54 per cent of areas respectively fell within this 10 per cent range of variation. If a maximum variation of 15 per cent is permitted, these figures are raised to 74, 73, and 64 per cent respectively. Granted the fact that a large number of the original CDs were quite small, these figures are reassuringly high. It can be fairly suggested that at least in terms of these few dwelling characteristics the residential areas analysed in this study are not unduly heterogeneous compared with the original CDs from which they are derived.

The regrouping described above yielded a new series of 611 ACDs, with an average population of 3,080 persons. Since the component CDs themselves averaged 907 persons, a range in the size of the new residential units was inevitable. About three-fifths had populations between 2,500 and 3,499 persons, but only a few were smaller than 2,000 persons (2 per cent) or larger than 4,000 persons (3 per cent). Moreover, correlation analysis of the relationship between population size and seventy socioeconomic, demographic, and ethnic variables described in succeeding chapters indicated that the highest correlation was -0.08. The average correlation with all seventy measures (ignoring sign) was 0.03. Clearly differences in ACD size have no appreciable effect on the variables included in this study, and such variations as do exist have been effectively randomised.

These 611 residential units provide the basis of the present study. For each a wide range of population data is available. But because of the official requirement to preserve the anonymity of individual residents in such small districts only aggregate figures are tabulated by the Bureau of Census and Statistics. No crosstabulations of different characteristics are available for CDs. That is to say, while for each area we know the industrial distribution of the workforce and the ethnic origins of the population, it is impossible (at least for these small residential units) to discover the industries of persons of different ethnic origins. Such a crosstabulation is, however, available for the metropolitan area as a whole and can be used to check any inferences about individual characteristics that the aggregate residential data may suggest. Thus, if we discover an ecological correlation such that ACDs with high proportions of building and construction workers tend also to have many immigrants, we can use data for the Melbourne metropolitan area as a whole to see whether immigrants are overrepresented in this industry. In fact they are, and in this instance the individual correlation supports the ecological one.

Most of the information provided from the 1961 census for individuals is also available for CDs, with the exception of some data on dwellings and on occupation. The available data include summary statistics (by sex) of the ages of the population in each CD, their marital statuses, workforce characteristics, industrial distribution (but not occupations), religion, birthplace, nationality, period of residence in Australia of foreign-born persons, and some information on dwellings. Population densities were obtained from another source,* and distance from the city centre was also calculated. From these data a total of seventy social and demographic characteristics were derived, providing a detailed social profile of each area. A variety of statistical techniques was then employed to analyse the way in which these characteristics were distributed over the metropolis, to measure the extent of segregation and concentration, to identify clusters of variables the distributions of which seemed to vary systematically one with the other, to suggest general factors in terms of which these patterns could be meaningfully interpreted, and to develop a parsimonious and statistically efficient method whereby residential areas with similar profiles could be grouped into larger social areas. But before we turn to these substantive questions, the analytic framework by means of which some order can be imposed upon this myriad of discrete social facts needs to be discussed.

---

* Dr G. J. R. Linge of the Australian National University kindly provided the area in square miles of CDs in Melbourne, from which residential densities were then calculated.

2

The Framework of Analysis

Viewed individually, the numerous residential areas which go to make up the shape of a city exhibit a bewildering variation in their social characteristics. There are areas where the population consists largely of transients; there are immigrant ghettos, localities where only the rich live, and suburbs composed predominantly of young families in the early stages of the life cycle. The volume of statistics that can be assembled to document such differences in any large city is truly enormous. In the present study almost 50,000 data cards containing half a million discrete social facts were initially processed, quantities which illustrate the pressing need for selectivity in any analysis that goes beyond the useful but often undigested data presentation characteristic of some community fact books.

In other studies of urban social structure a variety of analytical techniques has been employed to overcome the problem of ordering such masses of statistical information. In traditional ecological studies of the spatial structure of urban areas, perhaps the most commonly used frame of reference has been Burgess's concentric zone hypothesis, which has provided the basis for a vast amount of empirical research. Early studies used five district zones—the central business district, the zone in transition, the zone of independent working men's homes, the zone of better residences, and the commuters' zone. But before long these gave way to an indefinite number of concentric zones located more or less arbitrarily at mile or half-mile intervals from the central business district. To test the Burgess hypothesis, census tract data were aggregated within each zone, and the variation between zones for one or more social characteristics was noted. Within-zone variation was typically ignored, and the hypothesis was held to be supported if the characteristics selected declined, or increased, regularly with increasing distance from the city centre—that is, conformed to a regular gradient pattern (Burgess 1925).

An alternative, and sometimes complementary, approach was to follow Hoyt's emphasis on axial differences in urban residential structure, and to test for sectoral rather than concentric patterns. This required the aggregation of areal data not by concentric zones but by arbitrary sectors extending from the centre of the city (Hoyt 1939). A number of studies have attempted to evaluate the relative explanatory power of Burgess's and Hoyt's views of the social differentiation of residential areas, but, as Anderson and Egeland have pointed out, the dependence (at least operationally) of both schemes on average values for large zones or sectors of the city has usually made it very difficult to assess precisely how much of the variation in residential patterns is actually accounted for by either scheme (Anderson and Egeland 1961).

The Burgess and the Hoyt schemes reduce the complexity of variation in the social characteristics of residential areas by employing very coarse and generalised areal units (zones or sectors). The aggregation of areas to form a smaller number of zones or sectors serves to focus attention on the variation between them rather than within them. Other studies less concerned with generalisations about spatial organisation sometimes adopt a different approach, in which little or no initial grouping of the areal units is attempted. Instead the social characteristics to be analysed are reduced by multivariate techniques of analysis (typically factor analysis) or by the *a priori* construction of summary indexes. Tryon's work on cluster analysis (1955) and Schmid's study of crime areas (1960a, 1960b) exemplify the application of factor analytic methods to urban data, while social area analysis illustrates the use of *a priori* indices (factor analytic tests of these indices have been subsequently conducted).

In general it seems fair to suggest that exponents of the first approach (i.e. a Burgess or Hoyt scheme) see the differential distribution of social characteristics primarily as a means of making statements about urban *spatial* structure, while exponents of the second approach (including myself) view the same data more as a means of making statements about social differentiation and urban *social* structure. Some studies, of course, combine an interest in both these questions (Schmid 1960a, 1960b; Anderson and Egeland 1961; McElrath 1962). Nonetheless the analytic distinction between these two approaches is worth making. It is also worth emphasising that the analysis of similar data does not necessarily indicate an identity of research objectives.

Historically the first of these two approaches can be largely identified with human ecology, the second with social area analysis. While any researcher into urban social structure must acknowledge an intellectual debt to the work of human ecologists, urban geographers, and land economists, '. . . our concern with problems of social differentiation and stratification has led us to a different kind of analysis, and our attention has been focussed on relationships of a different order than those considered by urban ecologists' (Shevky and Bell 1955:1).

For us what matters most is not that the spatial distribution of social characteristics in cities conforms to this, that, or some other spatial hypothesis, but that these spatial distributions, whatever precise geographical arrangement they take, reveal processes of social differentiation and stratification. While in the present study some comments will be made about spatial patterns, the primary interest is not in spatial patterns as such but in what those patterns can tell us about the social structure of the city. It is this interest which places the present study closer to the interests of social area analysis than those of human ecology.

Social area analysis

A basic orientation in social area analysis is that the structure and composition of modern industrial cities must be studied in relation to the containing society. 'The objective of the Los Angeles study . . . was to understand urban aggregations, not as isolated, self-contained units, but as parts of a wider system of relationships' (Shevky and Bell 1955:1). Shevky and Bell regarded this orientation as a significant departure among sociological studies of residential differentiation in American cities, which had tended to treat the city as a relatively self-contained dominant factor that could be understood independently of trends in the wider society. Thus a primary task in social area analysis was to specify the nature and consequences of emergent structural changes in modern industrial societies.

In identifying master trends of recent social change Shevky and Williams (1949:Ch. 1) structured their analysis in terms of changes in economic organisation (relying mainly on Colin Clark's paradigm of economic growth), the theory of the demographic transition towards lowered fertility and smaller families, and changes in population distribution resulting from internal and international migration. It is of some importance to note that in this initial statement these general trends are discussed simply as a framework within which their detailed study of Los Angeles assumes a broader meaning, and the development of three general indices of social rank, urbanisation, and segregation is only loosely articulated with these general trends. In later formulations, however, these trends are viewed more generally as aspects of increasing societal scale, and a systematic attempt is made to forge stronger theoretical links between this specific method of urban analysis and a theory of social change.

The concept of scale is derived explicitly from the work of two social anthropologists, Godfrey and Monica Wilson (1954). By the scale of a society the Wilsons meant '. . . the number of people in relation and the intensity of these relations' (p. 25). In developing such a concept the Wilsons were, of course, following a classical tradition in sociological theory, and related distinctions, such as Tönnies's *Gemeinschaft* and *Gesellschaft* and Durkheim's mechanical and organic solidarity, immediately come to mind. The concept of societal scale owes even more to Durkheim's 'social density' and is equally difficult to define. Although the Wilsons attempt in a long discussion to give a precise content to the words 'intensity of social relations' it is probably fair comment that as they define it the concept of societal scale has little explanatory power. Many propositions about changes in scale turn out on closer inspection to be truismatic, such as their statement that '. . . all social change involves some change in scale' (Wilson and Wilson 1954:132). This merely asserts that social change occurs. Nadel (1953:102) has noted similar difficulties with this concept, and it remains to be shown that its use clarifies the analysis of social change. Perhaps this partly explains its failure to gain wide currency in sociological analyses. However, in social area analysis the concept of increasing societal scale has been used mainly as a shorthand equivalent for the processes of urbanisation, industrialisation, and modernisation (McElrath 1968:32-3, 36). Perhaps for the moment we can leave this tantalising concept at an intuitive level.

As already indicated Shevky and Bell identify three interrelated trends relevant to their discussion of recent social change: changes in the distribution of skills and in occupational patterns, changes in life style associated with the demographic transition and the changing economic functions of the household, and changes in the composition of the population because of migration. These trends appear to them to be most descriptive of the changing character of modern industrial society. They provide some documentation of the importance of these trends and go on to argue that given social systems can be viewed as standing in differential relationships to them at different times. More significantly in the present context, they further state:

> subpopulations in a particular society at a given point of time also can be conceived as standing in differential relationships to these three sets of structural changes . . . Thus, from certain broad postulates concerning modern society and from the analysis of temporal trends, we have selected three structural reflections of change which can be used as factors for the study of social differentiation and stratification . . . These factors are social rank, urbanization, and segregation (Shevky and Bell 1955:1-2).

Unfortunately this apparently smooth transition from certain broad postulates about changes in social structure to 'subpopulations' in general and census tracts in particular presents some important questions. For example, the bulk of Shevky and Bell's theoretical discussion about social change is largely concerned with total societies, or at least large geographic regions. It is therefore somewhat surprising when an empirical problem is selected for detailed analysis that the units of analysis are not nations, regions, or even cities, but census tracts within cities. Similarly the problem requiring explanation shifts from social change and social differentiation *per se* to the process whereby socially differentiated groups become clustered and residentially segregated within large cities. By implication their earlier discussion is viewed as contributing to our understanding of this process of residential differentiation. But although some passing remarks are offered to suggest why socially dissimilar groups tend also to have different locations within the city (Shevky and Williams 1949:61-2), none of the available theoretical statements about social area analysis recognises explicitly the implications of this shift of focus, a deficiency remarked upon by numerous critics of the method.* It is possible, for instance, to accept Shevky and Bell's propositions about social differentiation in modern industrial society, including their proposed constructs and empirical indicators, to admit their utility in comparing total societies, regions, and cities, but yet to ask why these three constructs should be useful in analysing residential patterns of social differentiation within cities. In short, their theory fails to indicate how the transition can be made from a theory of social change to a (largely unspecified) theory of residential differentiation.

In an interesting discussion of this and other points, Udry (1964) has made the same criticism, and the reply by Bell and Moskos (1964) is of some interest. They do not agree that this theoretical difficulty exists, and say (I paraphrase their reply): 'Take census tracts as units. Make repeated measurements on their populations over time and certain trends appear. These trends provide differentiating variables for the units under analysis. Our three measures were derived by using just such a logic.' Three comments seem appropriate. First, this argument suggests that the three constructs of social rank, urbanisation, and segregation were arrived at *inductively*; it does not answer the question whether they can be *deduced* from a theory of increasing scale. Second, the empirical validity of the three constructs used for measuring census tract differentiation is not at this point in question. In fact it has been shown that they can be fruitfully applied to a number of North American

---

* The construct of segregation is explicitly defined in spatial terms and is therefore a partial exception to this criticism.

cities, to Rome (McElrath 1962), and to Melbourne, as the present study attempts to show. The question is rather whether Shevky and Bell's discussion of social differentiation in urban industrial society has firm implications for the analysis of urban residential differentiation. Third, there is the question (not discussed by Shevky and his associates) why we should take census tracts as units of analysis at all. Social area analysis assumes that the census tract is a meaningful unit for sociological analysis without attempting any theoretical account of its importance. This is a surprising omission in view of the long discussion in human ecology of the appropriateness of the census tract as a unit in sociological analysis. Interestingly enough Tryon (1955:1-2, 38-44), whose analyses of census tract differentiation in San Francisco were familiar to Shevky and his colleagues, devotes considerable attention to this issue. Shevky and Bell, however, nowhere specifically state the reasons underlying their choice of census tracts in the analysis of social differentiation. They argue rather by analogy: urban subpopulations (census tracts) are like other subpopulations (cities, regions, nations), and all subpopulations can be studied in terms of the same constructs. Although it may be possible to expand upon such an argument, it would seem to carry little immediate force. At least one empirical study suggests that different constructs may be required to explain differences in the social characteristics of geographic units of different type (Udry 1964:413), and Simmel (1902) over sixty years ago argued that the internal differentiation and structure of a social system is partly a function of its size.

There is, however, a more direct demonstration that the relationship between the theory of social change and the differentiation of urban residential areas cannot be as straightforward as the available statements by social area analysts suggest. If social rank, urbanisation, and segregation are interrelated trends reflecting processes of societal change, then a legitimate expectation is that all three measures should be positively correlated in the statistical sense. Subpopulations with high values on one measure should also have relatively high values on the other two. Indeed, comparative data for different countries show that these general trends are related in this way, and McElrath (1968: 38) has recently concluded from data for thirty-eight countries that '. . . variations [in nine measures of social structure] are *closely related to a single factor*, which is here interpreted as the organizational scale of the society'.

When we come to analyse the social characteristics of census tracts this expectation fails conspicuously. Although in Los Angeles and the San Francisco Bay region in 1940 and 1950 social rank and urbanisation were positively correlated, from a slight to only a moderate degree (coefficients ranging from + 0·13 to + 0·41), social rank and segregation were somewhat more strongly, but negatively, related (Shevky and Bell 1955:27-9). That is to say, areas with high levels of social rank tended to have low levels of segregation. Data for Melbourne reveal a similar relationship. Thus, census tract data do not uniformly or consistently confirm propositions about changes in societal scale. How is this apparent contradiction to be resolved?

Let us first recapitulate the argument so far. By suggesting that the same three constructs—social rank, urbanisation, and segregation—can be applied without modification to geographic units of different type (tracts, cities, regions, countries), Shevky and Bell seem to imply that each and every subpopulation, however defined, can vary in scale. They state, for example, that although most of the published work to date has dealt with the census tract as the unit of analysis, 'there is no reason . . . why a typology based on the three social dimensions . . . could not be utilised . . . for the study of cities with the city as the unit of analysis, for the study of regions, or even for the study of countries' (p. 20). But does this mean that just as we might speak of the increasing scale of a country we can also speak of the increasing scale of a census tract? Clearly such an interpretation is not systematically adopted in their own work, since with the units selected for analysis (census tracts) the correlates of scale do not in fact correlate in the hypothesised way.

One solution to this dilemma lies in clarifying the concept of societal scale. The concept of scale, whatever its precise meaning, clearly applies to relatively inclusive social systems, that is to say to communities— social systems within which individuals can have most of the experiences and conduct most of the activities that are important to them in their day-to-day lives. Communities defined in this way differ in terms of scale (the range of interdependence) from village communities to towns, cities, regions, countries, and ultimately the world community. However, as argued in the preceding chapter, census tracts are not communities in this sense but only partial segments of the urban community. They do not themselves vary in scale. They do, however, reflect the scale of the urban community and of the total society of which they form part, since the effects of changing societal scale are pervasive. Perhaps this is all that the phrase 'structural reflections of change' really means. Viewed thus propositions about changes in societal scale lead to the identification of significant dimensions of social differentiation in a community, but it does not necessarily follow that these same dimensions will provide the bases for the residential segregation of social groups. The extent to which and the manner in which these dimensions of social differentiation may give rise to residential differentiation of socially dissimilar groups requires separate consideration. Constructs applicable to the macro-analysis of societal change may not be applicable, without modification, to the micro-analysis of residential differentiation in modern industrial cities.

In making the above criticisms of social area analysis, I should make it clear that I am partly addressing interpretations offered by more strenuous critics of the method. Although the early claims made in the name of social area analysis may have been too optimistic, it is equally clear that it has made a major contribution to the sociological study of urban phenomena. The identification, by whatever means, of three basic dimensions of social differentiation—social rank, urbanisation, and segregation—has proved to have wide applicability in studies of urban-industrial society, and encourages us to seek further development of these methods. In what follows I propose to accept Shevky and Bell's discussion of the major trends in recent social change not as a formal theory dictating the lines of subsequent analysis of urban residential differentiation,* but rather as a set of sensitising concepts directing attention to basic forms of social differentiation in modern industrial society, a view which seems quite consonant with their original intentions. Seen in this way, postulates about increasing societal scale constitute a conceptual scheme within which changes in social differentiation and stratification can be analysed. Granted that this analytic scheme in fact identifies basic dimensions of social differentiation, it is perfectly reasonable to anticipate that they may have consequences for the study of residential areas, for reasons which we now explore.

Social differentiation and residential patterns

In Australia, as in the United States and other highly industrialised countries, the rapid urbanisation which has occurred during the last century has been associated with long-term shifts in the relative distribution of the workforce between the primary, secondary, and tertiary sectors of the economy. In the present century, for example, the proportion of Australia's population living in metropolitan areas in-

---

* The interpretation of social area analysis as a self-proclaimed formal deductive system probably arises out of a diagrammatic presentation of argument from broad postulates to constructs and derived measures (Shevky and Bell 1955:4). Arrows are used to indicate the direction, but not the logical form, of the argument from broad generalisations to specific indicators. Shevky and Bell nowhere suggest it is a deductive system, but simply call their constructs 'structural reflections of change', a phrase which unfortunately permits a wide variety of interpretation.

C

creased from 35 per cent in 1901 to 56 per cent in 1961. Australia is today one of the most highly urbanised nations in the world. Over the same period the proportion of workers in primary industry declined from 33 per cent of the workforce to only 12 per cent, while the percentages in manufacturing and tertiary industries have steadily increased, as the following figures indicate (Jones 1967a; Farrag 1964). Even in 1901, however, the percentage of workers in tertiary industry was already high, reflecting in part the high level of urbanisation in Australia at that time.

Census year	Primary industry	Secondary industry	Tertiary industry	Total
1901	33	26	41	100
1911	30	29	41	100
1921	26	31	43	100
1933	24	32	44	100
1947	18	37	45	100
1954	15	39	46	100
1961	12	39	49	100

Following Shevky and Bell, changes in economic structure can be viewed in terms of the changing nature of social stratification in industrial society. Increasing division of labour and specialisation in occupational tasks, together with increasing levels of skill and education, have led to a hierarchical regrouping of occupations. Occupation comes to have a determining influence on status and rank, since the differential evaluation of occupational tasks is associated with inequalities in the distribution of the material and symbolic marks of economic success—income and prestige (Beshers 1962:57-60, 87-108). At the same time the increasing size of population aggregates and residential mobility limit severely the range of mutual social relations possible among urban inhabitants. Social standing is measured not by an intimate evaluation of persons and groups but by external and readily accessible indicators. In large cities one of the most important of these indicators is the residential area, as many studies of the social stratification systems of Western towns and cities have shown. Warner's use of the dwelling area as a component indicator in his Index of Social Characteristics (Warner *et al.* 1949:121-30), Hollingshead's adoption of a residential scale in his Index of Social Position (Hollingshead and Redlich 1958), and the dimensions of Social Rank in social area analysis all recognise the importance of place of residence in estimating a person's general social status.

The importance of residence as an indicator of social position derives from several sources. Housing is an essential, public, and expensive item of consumption. Where a person lives reflects not only the level of his income but also his values and his preferences. Especially in Australian cities, where the overwhelming majority of residents own the houses in which they live—in Melbourne in 1961, eight out of ten private householders owned or were purchasing their residences—the choice of a residential area conspicuously displays for most householders their economic position, the amount of their disposable income, their life style, and their pattern of expenditure.

Moreover, the very size of modern cities imposes constraints upon social interaction, and there is a tendency for persons with similar incomes, social positions, and values to reside in relatively close proximity so that group interaction can be maximised and group norms maintained. Over time the different residential areas of a city acquire a social evaluation reflecting the aggregate social characteristics of their resident populations, and as Robert E. Park (1952:177) succinctly observed spatial distance becomes an indicator of social distance. In short, the residential clustering of persons differentiated by levels of skill, income, and education (social rank) can be viewed as a function of differences in income, prestige, values, patterns of consumption, a presumed preference for neighbours with similar social characteristics, and a presumed rejection of neighbours with dissimilar characteristics. The extent to which such socioeconomic differentials are visible in the residential areas of modern industrial cities reflects the importance which occupation has come to have in determining the life chances and life style of urban industrial man.

Similar considerations apply to the concept of segregation. In Australia, as in many other countries, urban growth has resulted largely from internal and international movements of population. As the labour productivity of primary industry increases, its capacity to absorb additional workers declines. A large proportion of the surplus rural population is driven to seek employment in the expanding cities. When the demand for urban labour exceeds the natural growth of the workforce (and gains in labour productivity), as was typically the case in the countries of the New World, then the mass importation of workers and families from overseas countries of origin can serve to bridge the gap. Depending on the cultural distance of these immigrant streams from the host society, a greater or lesser degree of cultural diversity is introduced. In such culturally diverse and economically complex societies a person's ethnic or racial status becomes structurally important, as Warner *et al.* (1949:186-99) have shown for the United States, and Porter (1965:63) more recently for Canada. The same is undoubtedly true of Australia, where post-war economic growth has depended heavily upon an increasingly diverse stream of immigration. Especially in the cities of such culturally heterogeneous societies ethnic concentrations emerge, either positively, as a mechanism for maintaining established patterns of preferred and familiar ways of behaviour, or negatively, as a defence against discrimination and prejudice. Sometimes both factors reinforce each other. Once such concentrations have emerged, residential proximity serves to reinforce the characteristics of the subculture. In such societies, then, ethnic, racial, and other subcultural differences clearly constitute an important dimension along which urban residential areas become differentiated.

In suggesting how social differentiation along the dimensions of socioeconomic status and ethnicity becomes associated with the residential clustering of persons with similar social characteristics, we have so far considered the city primarily as a social system, as an aggregation of socially and culturally differentiated population groups and their places of residence. But the city also represents a complex spatial arrangement of economic activities. As the regional locus of economic and political power its basic facilities for production, exchange, and consumption—not least of all, its transportation and communication systems—must be so organised as to satisfy the needs and requirements of its resident population and of its hinterland as well. The territorial organisation of these basic urban facilities tends towards a typical pattern of land use, with the separation of industrial, commercial, residential, and recreational land uses.

Now, the individual residential areas of a city have a specific location with respect to these urban facilities, and differences in location determine access to them. As Garrison *et al.* (1959:145-6) have noted,

> Since our society is a highly interdependent one, no family in an urban area today may obtain at its residential site all the things necessary for its existence. The members of the household must travel, and travel frequently, to other locations within the city in order to obtain both the sustaining and the social necessities of life. In order to minimize the time spent in this movement, the household should choose a residential site which has maximum accessibility to all these activities. The following may be readily noted: shopping, work, school, church, and recreation, all of which are directly involved in the day-to-day operation of the family unit.

In addition to the effect of location on access to such facilities, each residential area itself contains a variety of physical facilities, in the form of land, roads, services, and dwellings. These dwellings vary in age, structure and condition, and provide relatively fixed characteristics for classifying areas. Equally importantly they partially determine the social characteristics of later residents.

Without extending this line of argument further, it can be suggested that the residential areas of a city, differing in the type of residential accommodation they provide and in their accessibility to different urban facilities, represent an opportunity structure. Competition within this opportunity structure by households with different requirements and different demands on specific urban facilities tends to produce a residential clustering of households at different stages of the life cycle. Thus, young unmarried workers or couples without children may tend to select residences with ready access to the central business district, whereas couples with young children may prefer to live in areas with easy access to schools and playing fields. In other words, the residential clustering of specific household types in different parts of the city reflects the uniformity of location requirements among different population groups. This suggestion, that spatial differences in household composition can be viewed largely as the result of the association of changing household requirements at different stages of the life cycle with accessibility factors and physical characteristics of dwelling areas, would seem to be supported by Rossi's finding (1955:178) that a high proportion of residential mobility in cities is generated by shifts in family composition accompanying different stages of the life cycle. In offering this interpretation, however, I should point out that this more limited interpretation of the urbanisation construct differs considerably from that originally given by Shevky.

These constructs, then, provide the broad analytic framework of our study. Residential differentiation in Melbourne will be viewed in terms of three major dimensions—socioeconomic status (social rank), household composition (urbanisation), and ethnicity (segregation). This framework of analysis will not, however, be imposed without regard to the facts, and indeed one major question that will arise is how adequate it is in explaining residential patterns in an Australian city. There is no suggestion that social reality is uniquely and exhaustively explained by these three dimensions alone, but I have made an initial assumption that they will be more important than any others. In adopting this general approach my debt to the research of Shevky and his associates is clear. It should also be clear, however, that the theoretical perspective of the present study departs somewhat from the accepted (indeed, sometimes rejected!) method of social area analysis. How significant these departures really are will be easier to judge as more comprehensive theoretical accounts of social area analysis become available.

In terms of methodology, too, the present study differs from previous studies in social area analysis. Principal component analysis and the empirical identification of differentiating factors is preferred to the *a priori* construction of index measures, and a different and more sophisticated technique of classification has been adopted in developing a typology of residential areas. These modifications result partly from advances in research technology, notably the wide availability of extremely fast and large computers. But the abstract discussion of methodology can sometimes be dull, and for those who are interested these methodological differences can be explored more easily elsewhere. For the others, they should in any case become clear, or at least noticeable, from the substantive analysis of residential patterns of social differentiation in Melbourne, a subject to which we now turn.

3

Socioeconomic Status

Melbourne was founded on the banks of the River Yarra less than a century and a half ago by John Batman, a pastoralist from Tasmania in search of better lands. At first his enterprise was viewed with disapproval by the mother colony of New South Wales. But two years later, in 1837, Governor Bourke journeyed from Sydney to legitimate Batman's action, naming the new settlement Melbourne after the British Prime Minister of the day. He thought, however, that another small village opposite the mouth of the Yarra was destined for greater things, and named it Williamstown after the reigning monarch. Time has proved Batman's judgment sounder. Today Melbourne is a metropolitan capital of two millions, and Williamstown one of its suburbs.

Since these early days Melbourne's growth has fluctuated markedly. When Victoria was proclaimed a colony in 1851 her population numbered under 25,000. But in the same year gold was discovered, and within three years this number had trebled. Five years later a quarter of a million immigrants had reached Victoria, most of them via the port of Melbourne, and by the beginning of the next decade Melbourne, now more populous than its nearest rival, Sydney, was a wealthy and vigorous boom town of 140,000 persons. Melbourne at that time was noted for the hard-drinking habits of its population and for its social fluidity. Changes in fortune were often extreme, and the fortuitous discovery of gold was a quick route to wealth and position in an atmosphere of independence and social equality (Grant and Serle 1957; Briggs 1963:285-319).

Rapid growth continued throughout the 1860s until the mid-1870s, when a decline in the importance of gold and more rapid economic development in New South Wales saw a temporary lull in Victorian expansion. But the next ten years, the decade from 1880 to 1890, were to be the most spectacular in Melbourne's short history. These were the years of Marvellous Melbourne, the years that saw a land boom and financial expansion the drama and excitement of which exhausted the local supply of superlatives. By 1891 Melbourne, that 'Paris of the Antipodes' or 'Chicago of the South' (depending on the company), was a city of about half a million. In ten years its population had grown almost as much as in the preceding thirty years, and in terms of its annual rateable property it stood as the third greatest city in the British Empire, surpassed only by London and (just ahead) by Glasgow.

The story of Marvellous Melbourne, of its foundations and ultimate collapse in the bank failure of the 1890s, has been well told by chroniclers, journalists, and historians alike (Grant and Serle 1957; Briggs 1963; Finn 1888; Smith 1903; Twopeny 1883). For our purposes the following figures, comparing Melbourne's growth with that of her older competitor, Sydney, tell their own story. Compare, for example, Sydney's steadier rate of growth with the fluctuating fortunes of Melbourne, where periods of massive growth were followed by years of relative stagnation. But note also Melbourne's early dominance in the population structure of Victoria, with 42 per cent of the state's population even in 1891, a figure not reached by Sydney until thirty years later. The degree of metropolitan dominance is still more marked in Victoria than in New South Wales.

Year	Melbourne		Sydney	
	Population in '000s	% of state population	Population in '000s	% of state population
1861	140	26	96	27
1871	207	28	138	27
1881	283	32	225	29
1891	491	42	383	33
1901	502	41	497	36
1911	589	45	630	38
1921	766	50	899	43
1933	1,053	58	1,315	51
1947	1,293	63	1,646	55
1954	1,524	62	1,863	54
1961	1,912	65	2,183	56
1966	2,108	66	2,445	58

Source: Hall 1905; *Censuses of the Commonwealth of Australia*, 1911 to 1966.

What these figures do not show is that the pattern of urbanisation in eastern Australia does not easily fit the general Western experience of industrialisation and urban growth. As Butlin (1964:181-210) has shown, there was some industrial activity in the Australian colonies of 1860, but this accounted for a mere 5 per cent of total output. Yet by international standards Australia was already highly urbanised, with 40 per cent of her population living in towns. Apparently urbanisation stimulated industrial expansion rather than the reverse, although it is true that as manufacturing activity grew in importance it stimulated further urban growth. The causes of this high urbanisation in general and metropolitan dominance in particular reflect a combination of economic, political, and geographical factors. Australia was settled predominantly from Great Britain (already a highly urban society in the nineteenth century) and the political and economic dependence of the early colonies on the 'Mother Country' emphasised the role of major ports such as Melbourne and Sydney. The importance of intercolonial trade in the export of primary products such as gold, wool, and wheat and in the import of manufactured goods, the early development of centralised railway networks to move such goods to and from the major ports, and the concentration of natural resources into the east and south of the continent, all contributed to the growth of cities and the concentration of population into a small number of urban centres (K. W. Robinson 1962). By World War I primate cities, in each case a political capital and port, had emerged in every state except Tasmania, and to a lesser extent Queensland. Even in these states the capitals were still by far the most populous cities. According to the 1961 census 55 per cent of Australia's population lived in the six state capitals, and in Victoria, at that time the state with the highest degree of metropolitan dominance, 65 per cent of the population lived in Melbourne.

The metropolitan dominance of Melbourne is reflected in its changing industrial structure. A detailed study of these changes has been made by Sinclair (1964), and here we have space only for a broad outline. Primary production was never a major source of employment in the metropolis itself, and even in 1871 only 4 per cent of Melbourne's workforce were employed in this sector, a figure which has since declined to 1 per cent. With increasing industrialisation and the concentration of manufacturing activity in the city (Linge 1962:22), the last ninety years have seen a rise in manufacturing employment from 30 per cent of the workforce in 1871 to a peak of 41 per cent in the mid-1950s. Since then a relative decline to 39 per cent has occurred, reflecting in part the effect of the 1960-1 recession. A more important factor has probably been the impact of capital-intensive methods of production. In the tertiary sector, a number of minor changes occurred —small declines, for example, in the relative importance of building and construction employment, and transport, storage, and communication—but by far the most dramatic decrease was among personal service workers, from 18 per cent of the workforce in 1871 to only 6 per cent by 1961. The declining importance of this group, the largest source of female employment in the nineteenth century, has been partly offset by the transfer of workers into manufacturing industry, and by increasing numbers of clerical, administrative, and professional jobs. The public service and professional groups doubled in importance between 1871 and 1961 (from 8 per cent to 15 per cent of the workforce), a trend which reflects the increasing specialisation of occupational tasks, the rising importance of managerial and supervisory functions in a technologically more complex and economically more interdependent society, as well as centralisation of political power and administrative control in a dominant metropolis.

With the growth of population and the expansion of its economic base, Melbourne's residential structure has taken more definite form. In Melbourne of the 1860s some commentators claimed that it was clear enough where the working class lived, even if as yet there were no 'industrial' suburbs (Grant and Serle 1957:77). However, the indiscriminate subdivision of building lots and the jerry-building of the gold-rush days had already scarred Fitzroy, Collingwood, and other inner areas, laying the foundations of the slums of future years (Finn 1888: Vol. 1, 24-30). Much of this early development consisted of terrace housing, the universally accepted town house in a time when distances were measured by walking or horse transport. But with the development of the suburban railway system and its rapid extension during the land boom of the 1880s, the ideal of a suburban villa—*Rus in Urbe*—in such salubrious sections of the city as Kew, Hawthorn, Malvern, Armadale, Toorak, Balaclava, and to some extent Essendon, was held before the eyes of the commercial classes, white-collar workers, and the more prosperous artisans. Those with the means were enticed to blend the advantages of urban and rural life in suburbs

> Having Views of Surpassing Grandeur of both Land and Sea,
>   that quite baffle description overlooking
> Hobson's Bay, the Shipping, the You-Yangs, Steiglitz Mountains,
> the Dandenong Ranges, Malvern, Toorak and Surrounding Country
>   Together with
> That Prodigious Growth, that Stupendous and Most Marvellous
> Monument of British Pluck of Modern Times, exhibiting Energy,
> Enterprise and Progress, the development of only some thirty-
>   odd years,
> that would do credit to the Growth of Centuries, that are
>   almost incredible for so short a time
> THE CITY OF MELBOURNE and SUBURBS with its Colossal
> Establishments and Buildings, with its steeples, spires, and sur-
> rounding Palaces, that are most astounding to Visitors and Dis-
> tinguished Tourists without doubt destined to become the LONDON
>   and PARIS of the SOUTHERN HEMISPHERE*

* I am indebted to Mr G. Davison of the Department of History in the Research School of Social Sciences of the Australian National University for this reference from the *Vale Collection of Real Estate Maps*.

and Mr R. E. N. Twopeny, an observant English visitor to Melbourne in 1880, noted a fairly general social division of the population by residential areas. His advice to the stranger who wished to form an idea of Melbourne's wealth was

> to spend a week walking around the suburbs and noting the thousands of large roomy houses and well-kept gardens which betoken incomes of over two thousand a year, and the tens of thousands of villas whose occupants must be spending from a thousand to fifteen hundred a year. All the suburbs are connected with the town by railway. A quarter of an hour will bring you ten miles to Brighton, and twelve minutes will take you to St Kilda, the most fashionable watering-place. Within ten minutes by rail are the inland suburbs, Toorak, South Yarra, and Kew, all three very fashionable; Balaclava, Elsternwick, and Windsor, outgrowths of St Kilda, also fashionable; Hawthorn, which is budding, Richmond, adjacent to East Melbourne and middle class; and Emerald Hill and Albert Park, with a working class population. Adjoining itself are North Melbourne, Carlton, Hotham, and East Melbourne, all except the last inhabited by the working classes. . . . [cited in Smith 1903: Vol. 1, 305-6].

Since Twopeny's visit Melbourne's population has increased over sixfold. The passing of the years has brought changes in the character of many areas, and with urban growth numerous new suburbs have been added. Toorak, however, has maintained its position as Melbourne's premier residential district, and the general division between largely middle class suburbs south and east of the city and working class suburbs to the north and west remains broadly accurate. But these are matters which can be determined now with some accuracy.

In Australia the contemporary study of differences in socioeconomic status levels among urban residential areas is handicapped by the lack of entirely adequate statistics. The 1961 census did not include questions on grade of income or level of education, and although information on occupation was sought, it is unfortunately not available for collectors' districts. For this reason the present study is based upon a wide range of data on occupational status and industry orders, which, while obviously relevant, are not quite as informative as data distinguishing levels of skills and occupational types. In addition to data on occupational status and industry, one item on owner-occupancy and two 'education ratios' were included. The education ratios were calculated separately for males and females by expressing the number of full-time students fifteen years of age and over as a percentage of persons aged between fifteen and twenty. It was hypothesised that they would vary positively with the socioeconomic status of an area: the higher the education ratio in a given area (the larger the relative number of males and females receiving full-time education beyond the legal school-leaving age), the higher its socioeconomic status.

In total twenty-four potential measures of the general dimension of socioeconomic status were analysed. Table 3.1 lists them, together with some information on the extent to which these social characteristics varied from one area to another. For those who may be unfamiliar with these statistics we can use the first measure, the percentage of the male workforce who were employers, as an example. According to Table 3.1 the median value for this characteristic was 5·1 per cent; that is, half the 611 areas in the analysis had values greater than this and half fell below it. Moreover, one in four areas had values which exceeded 7·8 per cent (the first quartile) and another quarter fell below 3·4 per cent (the third quartile). In other words areas in the 'top quarter' had at least twice as many employers as areas in the 'bottom quarter'. The interquartile range (IQR, column 5) indicates the spread of values among the middle 50 per cent of residential areas, and, like the mean and standard deviation (columns 6 and 7), provides some indication of the relative spread of observations. These statistics reveal that some characteristics are more evenly dispersed throughout the city than others. The extent to which particular social categories are residentially concentrated in some areas rather than others varies considerably. Thus, a simple comparison between employers and self-employed male workers indicates that, whereas they represent roughly equal percentages of the male workforce in the city as a whole, there is considerably more variability in the first measure than in the second. Employers are more 'segregated' than the self-employed.

If the spread of observed values for any measure was symmetrical (equally dispersed above and below the middle observation), the median and the mean would be exactly the same. When the mean is greater than the median, the spread of observations is more marked at higher than average values, and when the mean is less than the median the spread is greater among low values. Most of the measures shown in Table 3.1 have asymmetrical residential distributions, with a tendency for a greater spread of observations at higher than average values. To take the education ratios as an example, areas with high education ratios tend to be further away from the middle area than those with low education ratios. One of the few measures with negative 'skew' is the owner-occupancy ratio: almost all areas have high proportions of owner-occupied houses, but in those few areas where renting is common (for example the inner suburbs and state housing settlements) many people rent their dwellings.

The final column of statistics shown in Table 3.1 provides a summary measure of the degree of residential concentration for each measure. This index (the Gini index) (Jones 1967b) has a fairly direct interpretation. Its theoretical range is from zero (no concentration or equal distribution) to one (complete concentration or unequal distribution). If every area in Melbourne had contained exactly the same percentage of employers, then this measure of residential concentration would have been zero. If, on the other hand, all the employers in the city had lived in a single geographical area to the exclusion of any other, then the index would have been one. The importance of this statistic is that it provides an overall measure of inequalities in the residential distribution of social characteristics. As such it facilitates comparisons between different characteristics in the same city, and between the same characteristic in different cities at different times. The degree of residential concentration largely determines the visibility of a social category in the city's social and residential structure, and for our purposes those characteristics which display a strong degree of spatial clustering are the most important ones. Of course, the visibility of any social category is also a function of its absolute size. A small group, though highly concentrated, may be less visible than a larger group with somewhat lower concentration. The Gini index, being a relative measure of concentration, does not take that into account.

The greatest degree of residential concentration among these twenty-four socioeconomic characteristics is shown by the primary industry group, with a Gini index of 0·75. In fact 60 per cent of male workers in this industry lived in only 50 ACDs located on the periphery of the urban area. This is hardly a surprising finding in an expanding metropolis. Several other characteristics—the education and owner-occupancy ratios, for example—display moderate degrees of residential concentration. Even with an index value of only 0·30, between one in four and one in five of the city's population would need to change their place of residence in order to produce a distribution with no concentration. If instead of the existing degree of residential concentration among workers in finance and property a situation was to be reached in which every area had 3 per cent of its male workforce in that category—not twice as many or half as few—then about 25 per cent of workers in that category would have to move into different areas of residence. With a Gini index of 0·50 this figure increases to over one-third; at 0·70 it rises to between half and two-thirds.

It would at this point be confusing to attempt to describe in any detail the individual distributional patterns of all twenty-four socioeconomic characteristics. Often their patterns overlap, and in some cases the measures may not be entirely valid measures of the dimen-

TABLE 3.1 Some statistics relating to the distribution of 24 socioeconomic status characteristics over 611 ACDs, Melbourne, 1961

(1) Characteristic	(2) First quartile	(3) Median	(4) Third quartile	(5) IQR[a]	(6) Unweighted mean	(7) Standard deviation	(8) Coefficient of concentration
1 % MWF[b] in employer status	7·8	5·1	3·4	4·4	5·9	3·7	0·35
2 % MWF in self-employed status	6·6	5·5	4·2	2·4	5·6	2·3	0·22
3 % MWF not at work	5·4	3·7	2·6	2·8	4·2	2·3	0·32
4 % male non-workers retired or of independent means	4·6	2·5	1·2	3·4	3·2	2·7	0·48
5 % MWF in primary industry	0·9	0·5	0·2	0·7	1·3	3·4	0·75
6 % MWF in manufacturing	43·5	37·1	32·5	11·0	38·3	8·0	0·18
7 % MWF in electricity, gas, and water services	3·4	2·8	2·3	1·1	2·9	1·1	0·20
8 % MWF in building and construction	13·1	11·0	9·1	4·0	11·2	2·9	0·16
9 % MWF in transport, storage, and communication	12·0	9·8	8·0	4·0	10·1	3·0	0·18
10 % MWF in finance and property	5·1	3·1	1·8	3·3	3·6	2·3	0·37
11 % MWF in commerce	18·1	15·3	13·1	5·0	15·7	3·8	0·16
12 % MWF in public authority	5·4	4·2	2·9	2·5	4·4	2·9	0·26
13 % MWF in business and community service	8·2	5·6	3·7	4·5	6·6	4·5	0·33
14 % MWF in amusements, hotels, etc.	4·8	3·5	2·6	2·2	4·0	2·6	0·27
15 % MWF in other industries	2·4	1·3	0·8	1·6	1·8	1·7	0·46
16 % FWF[c] in manufacturing	46·2	34·8	26·0	20·2	36·1	12·9	0·33
17 % FWF in finance and property	7·8	5·9	4·3	3·5	6·1	2·5	0·25
18 % FWF in commerce	23·2	20·1	17·0	6·2	19·9	4·4	0·16
19 % FWF in public authority	4·1	2·9	2·0	2·1	3·1	1·7	0·31
20 % FWF in business and community services	21·8	15·7	10·7	11·1	17·1	8·4	0·34
21 % FWF in amusements, hotels, etc.	12·0	9·3	7·4	4·6	10·1	3·9	0·25
22 % owner-occupied private houses	91·6	86·5	74·7	16·9	81·0	15·2	0·53
23 Male education ratio	42	28	20	22	32	16	0·42
24 Female education ratio	28	18	10	18	21	15	0·51

a IQR = interquartile range.   b MWF = male workforce.   c FWF = female workforce.

sion of socioeconomic status at all. No one would presumably deny the validity of employer as an index of socioeconomic status, but legitimate doubts may well be raised about some of the industrial categories, which cut across differences in occupational status and include workers with widely differing levels of skill. The manufacturing category, for example, includes managerial, clerical, and supervisory staff as well as craftsmen, process-workers, and labourers in the same branch of industrial activity.

In the absence of other Australian studies which might provide guidelines in the choice of such indicators of socioeconomic status, the question of validity is best resolved empirically in relation to 'criterion' measures. It is reasonable to hypothesise that the employer category, the education ratios, and the business and community services category (which comprises mainly professional and white-collar workers) are valid measures of socioeconomic status. It can be further assumed that variables the residential distributions of which follow a similar pattern are measures of the same dimension of differentiation. Perhaps the most effective means of establishing whether different measures have similar or dissimilar patterns of areal distribution is to calculate the correlations between each pair of variables. As we have for each residential area a socioeconomic profile comprising twenty-four different measures, a correlation coefficient can be computed to measure the extent to which the different characteristics are spatially associated. Do areas with many employers also have relatively large numbers of self-employed males, few unemployed, and high education ratios? Table 3.2, which shows the zero order correlations between all possible pairs of measures, is designed to answer such questions.

In illustrating the meaning of this table it may be more interesting to take one of the suggested criterion variables, the female education ratio (the last column of Table 3.2). Looking down the correlations in this column, we can see that some characteristics have quite similar residential distributions to this ratio, whereas others have dissimilar distributions. The sign of the coefficient (positive or negative) indicates similarity or dissimilarity, and the size of the coefficient reflects the closeness of the relationship. The higher its value, the closer the fit between them. If we concentrate our attention mainly on coefficients approaching 0·50 we can conclude that areas with high female education ratios tend to have high values for employers, self-employed, retired men, and those of independent means, men employed in finance and property, commerce, public authority, business and community services, women in finance and property, or business and community services, and the male education ratio. A high female educa-

TABLE 3.2 Intercorrelations between the residential distributions of 24 socioeconomic status characteristics

	1	2	3	4	5	6	7	8	9	10	11	12	13	14	15	16	17	18	19	20	21	22	23	24
1 % MWF in employer status	100	69	-54	64	32	-67	-13	-30	-52	72	67	38	70	27	-42	-73	47	29	31	69	19	38	71	73
2 % MWF in self-employed status		100	-29	48	56	-60	-07	07	-31	46	40	16	51	33	-28	-48	31	22	17	47	11	28	42	44
3 % MWF not at work			100	-07	-21	38	-09	20	35	-66	-54	-53	-50	28	77	47	-61	-46	-28	-52	20	-66	-50	-54
4 % non-workers retired or independent means				100	08	-50	-15	-38	-22	47	47	21	48	51	01	-59	27	06	39	48	40	00	48	45
5 % MWF in primary industry					100	-39	-06	26	-33	20	04	10	26	-03	-23	-27	13	15	-06	20	-12	25	12	21
6 % MWF in manufacturing						100	08	16	20	-70	-63	-52	-76	-36	33	84	-44	-30	-39	-70	-24	-08	-52	-56
7 % MWF in electricity, gas, and water services							100	34	06	03	-02	-01	-12	-19	-13	11	24	19	-06	-08	-24	19	-09	-05
8 % MWF in building and construction								100	12	-26	-35	-22	-27	-13	06	39	-12	03	-38	-28	-27	06	-36	-31
9 % MWF in transport, storage, and communication									100	-35	-28	-10	-35	05	30	36	-17	-10	06	-36	00	-33	-42	-45
10 % MWF in finance and property										100	78	60	73	17	-61	-77	67	51	45	74	12	40	65	68
11 % MWF in commerce											100	48	60	21	-51	-68	62	58	45	65	30	23	60	57
12 % MWF in public authority												100	56	14	-45	-60	48	34	47	44	-14	23	37	45
13 % MWF in business and community services													100	34	-39	-83	45	16	41	75	04	22	63	64
14 % MWF in amusements, hotels, etc.														100	21	-36	-04	-17	25	16	37	-37	16	13
15 % MWF in other industries															100	37	-56	-54	-21	-44	15	-58	-41	-45
16 % FWF in manufacturing																100	-52	-30	-50	-77	-20	-14	-63	-68
17 % FWF in finance and property																	100	60	42	49	02	37	42	46
18 % FWF in commerce																		100	23	31	14	25	24	28
19 % FWF in public authority																			100	39	17	02	34	35
20 % FWF in business and community services																				100	25	24	67	66
21 % FWF in amusements, hotels, etc.																					100	-34	20	12
22 % owner-occupied private houses																						100	36	39
23 Male education ratio																							100	70
24 Female education ratio																								100

tion ratio also tends to be associated with a low percentage of unemployed males, few men in manufacturing or transport, storage, and communication, and a low percentage of women engaged in manufacturing industry.

These systematic patterns of association are not, of course, unexpected, but conform to expectations suggested by our discussion of stratification in urban-industrial society. Some reflect the impact of individual relationships, such as the high positive association between the percentage of employers and the percentage of men in business and community services. The percentage of employers in this industry group is relatively high (14 per cent, compared with only 6 per cent in the metropolitan male workforce as a whole). Other relationships, such as the high negative association between the education ratios and women working in manufacturing industry, reflect unit (ecological) rather than individual correlations, in this case the tendency for areas of high socioeconomic status to havē few women working in this presumably low-status industrial category. In this connection it is worthwhile emphasising that correlation is not the same as causation. It would be nonsense to suggest that a low education ratio among teenage girls simultaneously causes *other* women to be employed in manufacturing. The negative correlation between these two variables most probably reflects a common cause. Areas where few girls are educated beyond the legal school leaving age tend to be areas of low socioeconomic status, where economic pressures and a low valuation of education combine to limit the level of education achieved by children. Adult women in the same areas probably have few skills and seek employment in factories. Thus a common cause (socioeconomic status) produces the observed relationship.

Although the individual correlations shown in this table are interesting in themselves, they also demonstrate the existence of systematic patterns of residential differentiation among these different measures. The residential distributions of several characteristics overlap considerably. The correlation coefficients for the education ratios, the percentages of employers and self-employed males, and several other variables are very similar one to another, both in direction and in size. But other variables, such as the percentage of unemployed* men or the percentage of women in manufacturing industry, tend to display quite different residential patterns. Instead of viewing the specific residential distributions of twenty-four different measures separately, can

---

* In Victoria as a whole in 1961, the 'not at work' category consisted mainly of unemployed males (67 per cent), but also included those temporarily laid off, sick, or otherwise unable to secure work.

we interpret them jointly in terms of more general factors of social and residential differentiation?

The most direct means of answering this question is by principal component analysis, a technique of multivariate analysis similar to factor analysis. Component analysis is mathematically less complex than factor analysis, however, and does not involve assumptions about simple structure and communalities (M. G. Kendall 1957; Seal 1964: 119-20, 167-9; Harman 1960:154-91; Cartwright 1965). This technique of analysis, which is well understood by statisticians, has been widely applied in social science research. In psychology it is more commonly known as the principal axes method of factor analysis and is routinely applied to derive an initial solution for rotation to simple structure. The innovation in this study lies not in the method itself but in its application, particularly in 'factoring' conceptually independent domains.

Component analysis begins usually from a correlation matrix such as Table 3.2, from which independent (uncorrelated) components or 'factors' are extracted by the mathematical technique of finding the latent roots (eigenvalues) of the matrix. These components re-express the observed correlations in a potentially more meaningful way. They are mathematical artefacts and consist of weights (sometimes called factor coefficients) which are established by the method of analysis and indicate the different contribution each original measure makes to a specific component. The first component extracted from the correlation matrix is that which explains the greatest variance among the original measures. The effect of this component is eliminated, and the next component, which accounts for the greatest amount of the remaining variance, is then extracted. This process continues until all the variance has been statistically explained. In the present case, with a correlation matrix for twenty-four primary variables, twenty-four components can be extracted. In practice, however, one is usually concerned only with the largest components, since these have the greatest explanatory power.

Table 3.3 shows the factor coefficients for the first three principal components derived from Table 3.2. They jointly account for 62 per cent of the original variance. In other words, almost two-thirds of the variance among the twenty-four original measures can be understood in terms of only three new constructs. The remaining twenty-one components not shown explain the remaining 38 per cent of the variance, and obviously are individually and collectively less important than those shown. Another reason for ignoring these lower-order components is that it is frequently difficult to interpret their meaning. The

TABLE 3.3 Factor coefficients between 24 socioeconomic status characteristics and three principal components (unities in the principal diagonal of correlation matrix)

Characteristic	Factor coefficients for components		
	Socio-economic status	Zone in transition	Urban fringe
1 % MWF in employer status	0·86	0·11	0·26
2 % MWF in self-employed status	0·61	0·09	0·56
3 % MWF not at work	−0·67	0·55	0·12
4 % male non-workers retired or of independent means	0·58	0·55	0·10
5 % MWF in primary industry	0·30	−0·20	0·71
6 % MWF in manufacturing	−0·80	−0·23	−0·15
7 % MWF in electricity, gas, and water services	−0·05	−0·45	−0·11
8 % MWF in building and construction	−0·34	−0·37	0·40
9 % MWF in transport, storage, and communication	−0·45	0·14	−0·44
10 % MWF in finance and property	0·90	−0·09	−0·13
11 % MWF in commerce	0·82	0·04	−0·27
12 % MWF in public authority	0·63	−0·12	−0·29
13 % MWF in business and community services	0·83	0·15	0·11
14 % MWF in amusements, hotels, etc.	0·23	0·73	0·07
15 % MWF in other industries	−0·61	0·58	0·10
16 % FWF in manufacturing	−0·88	−0·23	0·03
17 % FWF in finance and property	0·68	−0·31	−0·19
18 % FWF in commerce	0·48	−0·38	−0·30
19 % FWF in public authority	0·51	0·22	−0·47
20 % FWF in business and community services	0·83	0·10	0·01
21 % FWF in amusements, hotels, etc.	0·17	0·60	−0·12
22 % owner-occupied private houses	0·41	−0·66	0·17
23 Male education ratio	0·77	0·07	0·03
24 Female education ratio	0·80	−0·01	0·06
Eigenvalue (V_p)	9·83	3·17	1·94
100 $V_p/24$	40·96	13·21	8·08

influence of measurement and computational errors becomes progressively greater as increasingly less important components are extracted. Also, when the value of any component (eigenvalue) falls below one, it has less explanatory power than a single measure in the original series. In most cases any possible meaning it may have is intrinsically uninteresting. Generally speaking, the usefulness of component analysis (and factor analysis) lies in its capacity to suggest broad constructs the explanatory power of which far exceeds that of any single measure included in the study.

According to Table 3.3 the first component accounts for 41 per cent of the original variance and has very much greater explanatory power than the next largest component. By examining the pattern of factor coefficients associated with the first component (column 2) we can begin to interpret its meaning. These coefficients can most easily be understood if thought of as if they were correlation coefficients between each component and the original measures. They are measures of the importance or 'weight' of a particular variable in a specific component: the higher the coefficients (which cannot exceed one), the greater the importance of that measure for that component. From the coefficients in the second column of this table it is quite clear that this first component measures differences in socioeconomic status among the 611 residential areas in the analysis. It has high positive loadings on white-collar, commercial, and professional industry groups (variables 10, 11, 13, and 20), on the percentage of employers and the education ratios (variables 1, 23, and 24), but high negative loadings on blue-collar industry groups (variables 6 and 16) and the percentage of men not at work (mainly unemployed).

These factor coefficients not only enable us to interpret the meaning of a component. They can also be used as weights to calculate component scores for each area which can then be used as substitutes for the original measurements. Perhaps the simplest way of explaining the derivation of such scores is to consider the factor coefficients as though they were directions in a recipe. Thus, the second column of Table 3.3 can be read as follows: for each area take 0·86 of the percentage of employers, add 0·61 of the percentage of self-employed males, take away 0·67 of the percentage of men not at work, add 0·58 of the percentage of men not in the workforce who are retired or of independent means, add 0·30 of the percentage of men in primary industry, take away 0·80 of the percentage of men in manufacturing, and so on until all twenty-four measures and weights have been included. The size of the coefficient determines how much weight is given to a particular measure, and its sign determines the direction of the mathematical operation. An area with a high positive score on the first component is one with high socioeconomic status; an area with a low negative score has low socioeconomic status. Component scores, when calculated for all the different areas, can be used instead of the original measures to differentiate their relative standing along this dimension. When correlated with the original measures, they would turn out to be correlated 0·86 with the percentage of employed, 0·61 with self-employed males, − 0·67 with those not at work, and so on. In other words, the factor coefficients can also be interpreted as correlations between the primary variables and the component scores. To calculate component scores all variables are expressed in standardised form before scoring. Vector weights, not factor coefficients, are usually employed in the calculation of scores. Factor coefficients are mathematically related to vector weights, being in fact derived by scaling them by the square root of the associated eigenvalue (see Harman 1960).

Given the fact that all the measures shown on Table 3.3 were selected on the grounds that they were *prima facie* measures of socioeconomic status, it is only to be expected—indeed hoped—that the first principal component should reflect this dimension of residential differentiation. Component analysis, like factor analysis, is only an analytical technique (admittedly a mathematically very sophisticated one), and what the method discovers depends on the information given to it to analyse and on the assumptions implicit in the analysis. If different measures had been employed, somewhat different results might have emerged—how different would depend, in turn, on what these new measures were. But to admit this is not to suggest that the present results are arbitrary. What is true is that the adequacy of any solution is not basically a function of the method of analysis. Its adequacy depends much more on the initial formulation of the problem and the selection of measures. Even granted this degree of interdependence between the way a problem is specified and its ultimate solution, it is impressive that the socioeconomic status component emerges so dominantly. It is three times as important statistically as the second component, thereby suggesting that Shevky and Bell's identification of this factor as an important dimension of social and residential differentiation is reasonable and fruitful.

Although less important, the second and third components are nonetheless interesting, partly because they show that the twenty-four measures originally selected do not all capture differences in socioeconomic status. This results partly from the fact that virtually all the workforce characteristics available from the census were included. Some are clearly inadequate measures of socioeconomic status (variables 7, 8, 9, 18, and 21 fall into this category), presumably because some industry groups cut across meaningful divisions in socioeconomic status and occupational prestige. Some are more closely connected with the second component, which has been tentatively identified as a 'zone in transition' factor. The variables most closely associated with it are the percentages of workers in amusements and hotels, the owner-occupancy ratio, and to a lesser degree the percentages of men not at work and retired or independent. All these measures tend to be relatively centralised in their residential distribution: the values of the percentages concerned decline with increasing distance from the central business district.

When scores for the second component were calculated and mapped, those with high scores showed a tendency to cluster around the central city. These areas have low residential stability (low owner-occupancy ratios), high proportions of unemployed and retired or independent persons, and many workers in amusements, hotels, and related services (an industry with a high proportion of immigrant workers). This component seems to identify what Burgess called the zone in transition. It is very interesting to note that scores for this component correlate negatively ($r = -0.81$) with scores on a familism component described in the next chapter. In other words this zone in transition factor identifies areas with low familism. Perhaps some of these measures belong to the dimension of familism and not socioeconomic status, as I had first expected. If this is so, the dominance of the first component of Table 3.3 is even more impressive.

The third component, which explains only 8 per cent of the variance, has quite a clear interpretation: it differentiates the urban-rural fringe of the metropolis. By far its highest loading is on the percentage of men in primary industry. The second highest is on the percentage of self-employed, reflecting the relatively high proportion of self-employed workers in primary industry.

The discussion so far has had two general objectives. The first was to see whether a wide range of workforce and industry data selected from the 1961 census clustered in such a way as to justify an interpretation which viewed them as jointly reflecting an underlying dimension of social and residential differentiation, termed social rank by Shevky and his associates and identified here as socioeconomic status. The results of the component analysis reported above support such an interpretation, with the qualification that some of the industry categories included are not primarily related to this dimension. The second objective, dependent upon the first, was to derive a valid and reliable measure of the socioeconomic status level of an area. As explained above, the factor coefficients of Table 3.3 provide a means of obtaining such a measure, through the calculation of component scores. These scores summarise all the original measures included in the analysis, but each measure contributes differentially to the final score. The amount contributed by a given measure is determined by the factor coefficients, which are derived from the observed interrelationships among the original variables. I hope I have by now established to the reader's satisfaction as well as my own that this component analysis has provided us with a valid and reliable measure of socioeconomic status. Obviously additional information on income, land and dwelling values, and topographical features would have strengthened this part of the analysis. But such data would not, I think, have substantially modified our results. Those who feel that 'the proof of the pudding is in the eating' can perhaps test their judgment by evaluating the general picture of socioeconomic status differences that these component scores provide.

Socioeconomic status scores for all 611 ACDs are mapped on Fig. 1. For simplicity of presentation only five broad groups of scores are shown. The individual scores were ranked, from the highest to the lowest, and then the 'top' 20 per cent (122 areas with the highest scores), the second 20 per cent, third 20 per cent, and so on for all five groups of 20 per cent (quintile groups) were mapped in different hatchings. A list of the ACDs in each group is provided and the actual component scores are given in Appendix I.

Undoubtedly the clearest finding that emerges from this figure is that there is no systematic gradient in socioeconomic status. Although there is some tendency for socioeconomic status to increase with distance $(r = +0.32)$, most of the higher status areas are in the middle distance suburbs east and south of the central business district. These suburbs lie mainly in a largely continuous belt south of the River Yarra, which serves as a major line of social demarcation in the city, at least so far as its residential structure is concerned (Jones 1967c). In 1961 there were only a few areas north or west of the river which had higher than average socioeconomic status. Thus, in Melbourne sectoral differences seem more important than zonal differences in the location of areas of high socioeconomic status (Johnston 1966), although even east of the city centre the level of socioeconomic status declines along the outer reaches of the Melbourne-Dandenong railway line, reflecting in part the development of industry in this section of the city.

To illustrate concisely the range of differences in social characteristics between areas in the different groups, abridged social profiles of a few residential areas are given. Complete profiles for all areas are, of course, available, but cannot be presented here because of limited space. Table 3.4 shows for each of seven areas (the areas with the highest and lowest scores, and areas in the middle of each of the five groups) percentages for five selected characteristics. The areas are numbered according to the base map, and since they do not correspond to named localities, such as suburbs, I have given them generic titles only. These figures are only illustrative, but they tell a consistent story. The contrasts are fairly marked and reflect the extent to which differences in socioeconomic status divide, at least residentially, those who

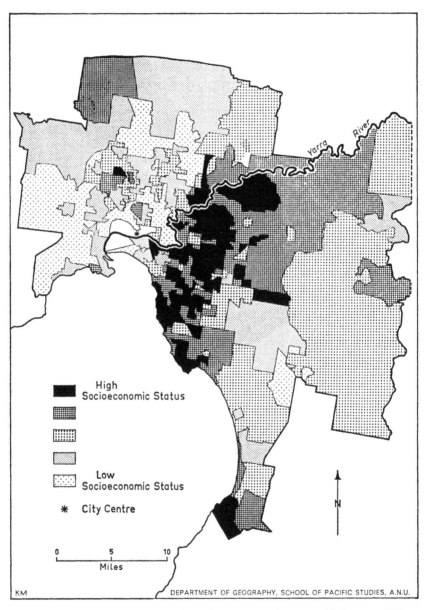

FIG. 1 The residential distribution of socioeconomic status, Melbourne, 1961

Key to Fig. 1

First quintile group (high socioeconomic status)

1	45	95	108	126	141	294	312	374	478
2	46	96	109	127	243	295	313	376	481
21	47	97	110	128	250	296	314	406	501
24	48	98	111	129	251	297	315	407	505
34	49	99	112	132	252	298	316	408	506
35	69	100	113	133	263	299	317	409	545
36	70	101	114	134	264	300	322	470	548
37	89	102	115	135	265	304	323	472	550
39	90	104	116	136	266	305	331	473	576
41	91	105	119	138	290	306	332	474	578
42	92	106	120	139	291	310	346	475	602
43	93	107	123	140	293	311	347	476	603
44	94								

Second quintile group

14	117	199	258	321	344	377	461	504	572
22	122	200	262	324	345	378	462	507	574
23	124	201	288	325	348	379	463	509	575
26	125	202	289	327	349	380	464	514	577
27	130	203	292	328	350	381	465	536	579
28	131	239	301	329	351	382	466	538	580
29	137	242	302	330	369	383	467	543	584
30	142	245	303	333	370	384	468	544	587
32	143	246	307	334	371	420	469	546	596
33	171	249	309	341	372	421	471	547	598
38	173	253	319	342	373	422	479	559	600
40	192	254	320	343	375	460	503	569	607
103	193								

Third quintile group

18	144	188	256	308	357	411	480	549	590
19	145	189	257	318	363	418	484	566	591
25	146	195	259	326	385	423	492	570	592
31	148	196	260	335	392	430	502	571	593
51	149	204	267	336	394	431	508	573	594
52	154	205	268	337	395	438	510	581	595
56	163	208	269	338	396	440	511	582	597
68	168	240	270	339	397	441	512	583	599
78	169	241	274	340	398	442	513	585	601
80	170	244	277	352	399	444	515	586	606
86	172	247	282	353	400	447	516	588	608
118	186	248	283	354	410	477	539	589	610
121	187	255							

Key to Fig. 1—*continued*

Fourth quintile group

3	88	164	220	278	386	417	482	498	553
5	147	165	221	280	387	419	483	499	554
7	150	166	222	281	388	425	486	500	555
8	151	167	223	355	389	426	487	525	556
10	152	185	224	356	390	427	488	526	557
15	153	190	226	359	391	428	489	531	558
17	156	194	230	360	393	429	490	532	560
50	157	197	233	364	401	433	493	533	564
55	158	198	235	365	412	439	494	537	565
67	159	206	236	366	414	445	495	540	604
77	160	207	237	367	415	446	496	541	605
81	161	209	261	368	416	448	497	542	609
83	162								

Fifth quintile group (low socioeconomic status)

4	60	79	180	216	271	362	443	485	529
6	61	82	181	217	272	402	449	491	530
9	62	84	182	218	273	403	450	517	534
11	63	85	183	219	275	404	451	518	535
12	64	87	184	225	276	405	452	519	551
13	65	155	191	227	279	413	453	520	552
16	66	174	210	228	284	424	454	521	561
20	71	175	211	229	285	432	455	522	562
53	72	176	212	231	286	434	456	523	563
54	73	177	213	232	287	435	457	524	567
57	74	178	214	234	358	436	458	527	568
58	75	179	215	238	361	437	459	528	611
59	76								

live in the metropolis. Areas near the bottom are clearly some social, as well as geographical, distance from those near the top. It should be no surprise to anyone who has thought seriously about the structure of Australian cities that a fringe area ranks so low. The slums in the decaying heart may attract more attention—they are seen by more people—but the problems facing young families on low incomes in new industrial suburbs are equally pressing. Distance and segregation from more affluent areas mask, but do not reduce, such difficulties.

TABLE 3.4 Abridged socioeconomic status profiles of seven residential areas, Melbourne, 1961

Area	% MWF in employer status	% MWF not at work	% MWF in business and community services	% FWF in manufac- turing	Female education ratio
299 (stately homes)	24	1	24	9	71
472 (fashionable beachside)	10	2	10	25	41
536 (suburban middle)	5	2	9	28	25
395 (suburban middle)	5	3	5	37	19
223 (inner industrial)	3	3	3	50	11
73 (old industrial)	3	7	3	56	3
562 (fringe industrial)	1	7	1	58	5

How marked, in comparative terms, was residential clustering by socioeconomic status level in Melbourne in 1961? It is not particularly easy to give a firm answer to this question. Other studies have not always used a similar framework of analysis or produced similar statistics. Moreover, the measurement of residential concentration itself poses problems. For example, differences in the size of the units of analysis influence results. However, Duncan and Duncan (1955), in a study of 1950 data for Chicago, found that the degree of residential concentration was greatest among professional and technical workers at one end of the occupational scale, and labourers at the other (Gini indexes of 0·30 and 0·35 respectively). A comparison with indexes shown on Table 3.1 suggests that the degree of residential clustering by socioeconomic status level in Melbourne in 1961 was not markedly different from that in Chicago in 1950. But to the extent that the areas in the present study are smaller than American census tracts, we would expect somewhat higher indexes for Melbourne. Comparative Australian data are not available but there is no reason to believe that Melbourne is atypical in its degree of residential concentration compared with other Australian metropolises.

The implications and effects of residential segregation are best discussed after examining other dimensions of spatial differentiation as well. It may be that the concentration of groups differentiated by socioeconomic status level is less marked than it is for other characteristics, such as household type and ethnic origin. Certainly the quantitative indexes of concentration shown in Table 3.1 suggest that residential concentration according to industry group and workforce status is moderate rather than extreme. But equally they demonstrate the existence at the neighbourhood level of substantial socioeconomic differentials in an Australian metropolis. Broadly speaking, however, it seems that although Melbourne's residential areas are differentiated in terms of the collective socioeconomic status of their residents, they differ just as much if not more in terms of their household and ethnic characteristics. But this generalisation can be more readily evaluated from subsequent analysis.

4

Household Composition

The analysis presented in the preceding chapter disclosed a marked concentration of areas with higher than average socioeconomic status in districts east and south of the city centre. This concentration, which was noted in an earlier report on Melbourne's residential structure (Melbourne and Metropolitan Board of Works 1954:29-42, 49-68), has to be viewed against the background of differences in the natural environment in the city. During the past sixty or seventy years, the rate of new residential development has been much more rapid in the eastern and southern suburbs than in the north and west, for reasons which seemed obvious enough to the authors of Melbourne's 1954 *Planning Scheme* report.

> The proximity of the bayside beaches, the lighter soil and gentle slopes have all contributed to the popularity of the southern district. In the east, the lighter, more undulating terrain, while adding somewhat to building costs, has resulted in many delightful residential areas which, added to the proximity of the pleasant hill country further out, have had an increasing attraction for home seekers. In the west, on the other hand, the country is flat, windswept and barren, the soil heavy and tenacious, the rainfall low, and generally the area is more suited for industrial than residential use. The north, while more attractive than the west, has not the appeal of the east and south. (p. 49)

The extent of these preferences can be seen clearly from Fig. 2, which depicts in a generalised way the pattern of residential development in Melbourne over the past eighty years. The map shows this growth in relation to the 1961 metropolitan boundary, and the slower rate of residential expansion west and north of the city centre is immediately apparent. The main lines of development have been along transportation routes extending some distance east and south of the central business district, with rapid infilling of the interstitial areas in each successive period of growth.

But the pattern of residential development has also to be seen in relation to the disposition of industrial activity in the city. The most notable concentrations of manufacturing are in the central city itself, or rather south of the central city between the River Yarra and Port

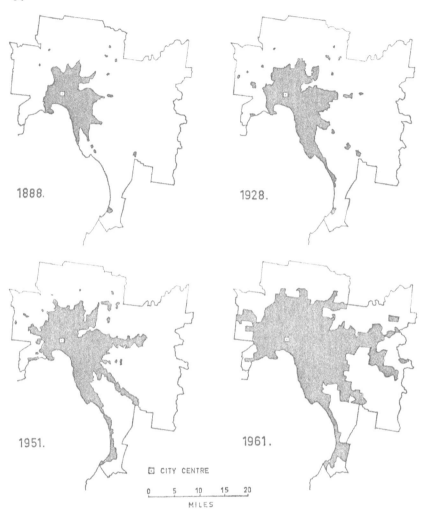

FIG. 2   The pattern of growth, Melbourne, 1888-1961

Phillip Bay, but there is also substantial industrial activity west of the Maribyrnong River, in Footscray, Newport, Altona, and, further north, Sunshine. Fig. 3 shows the location of major industrial concerns in Melbourne in the early 1960s. The concentration of manufacturing activity is most marked in the central, western, and northern sectors of the city, although even in the east and south some recent industrial development has occurred. However, the higher status areas are on the whole relatively free of industrial activity. This separation reflects not only a tendency towards the residential segregation of white-collar from blue-collar workers, but also the tendency for major industrial complexes to locate in areas (not always central) least in demand as sites for residential development. Admittedly, the relationship between non-residential and residential land uses is very much more complicated than this simple statement suggests. But the extent of this process of growth and separation can be seen from the fact that in 1951 almost 85 per cent of jobs were located in the central, northern, and western sectors, whereas two-thirds of the city's population lived in the southern or eastern sectors. Planning since that time has been aimed at encouraging industrial development south and east of the city and at achieving a more balanced relationship between residence and place of work (Melbourne and Metropolitan Board of Works 1967:8).

The pattern of any city's growth is captured more or less permanently in physical and demographic terms, in the age and condition of its housing, and in the family characteristics of people living in different parts of the city. The oldest sections tend to have the oldest populations and the newest areas the youngest, so that the average age of the population tends to decline the further one goes from the centre of the city. But even more important than differences in the age of the houses and the people who occupy them is the concentration of workers in the inner city districts. Of all the characteristics considered in this chapter, the one most strongly related to distance from the central business district (CBD) is the dependency ratio—the number of dependants relative to the number of workers. This ratio increases very markedly with increasing distance from the CBD, a trend which reflects the continuing importance of the central city in the employment structure of the metropolis. But while it remains the single most important employment centre in Melbourne, its relative position has been declining. Since 1951 employment in the CBD has been virtually stable at about 150,000 to 160,000 workers, whereas employment elsewhere in the metropolitan area has increased by over half. By 1961 only 19 per cent of the metropolitan workforce were employed in the CDB, compared with 25 per cent in 1951. The importance of these trends will become clear from the analysis that follows.

Following Shevky and Bell, this section of our analysis is structured according to the expectation that different parts of the city will vary systematically in household composition. There are areas where unmarried working adults predominate, areas with high proportions of the widowed, separated, and divorced, as well as areas where the typical household consists of a conjugal family in the early stages of the life cycle. To identify such differences a wide range of census

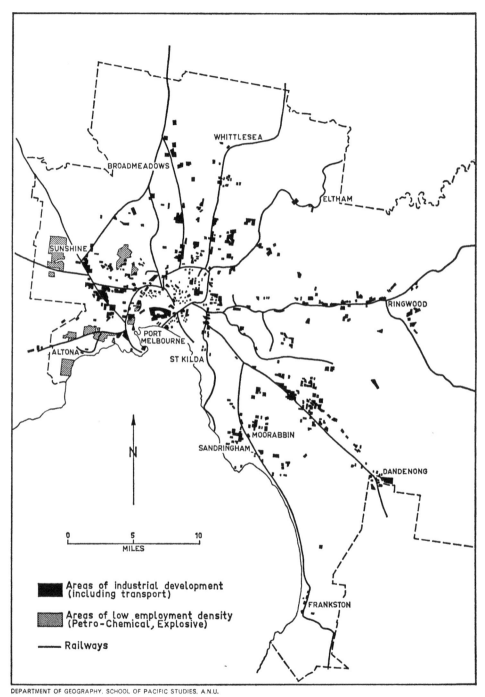

FIG. 3 The location of industry in contemporary Melbourne

characteristics relating to these characteristics was analysed, not so much because of an interest in individual variables as such, but mainly as a means of arriving at a reliable and discriminating measure of household type.

The variables considered in this section are presented in Table 4.1. Most of them require little explanation. Some relate to the type of dwellings in each area, and distinguish dwellings occupied by a single household from those which are shared by more than one household, and from those consisting of flats, rooms and apartments, and non-private dwellings (boarding-houses, hotels, guest houses, and the like). A complete age-profile of each area is also given, distinguishing dependent children from teenagers and young adults, persons in the prime of life from those approaching middle age or retirement. By relating the number of children under five to the number of women of childbearing age (the so-called fertility ratio), an estimate of fertility differentials within the city can also be obtained. It was also anticipated that differences in rates of population growth and residential densities would be related to differences in household composition, since the most recently settled areas have young populations and relatively low densities, reflecting the Australian preference for separate houses standing on their own lots. The reasons for including information on marital status are also clear enough, and workforce participation rates throw additional light on family structure.

Some explanation, however, may be required for including pensioners in this section, as persons of independent means (including retired) were included in the dimension of socioeconomic status. There were two reasons for this decision. Pensioners consist predominantly of old-age pensioners, whereas persons of independent means have a wider age spread. Secondly, persons of independent means can be reasonably assumed to be of higher than average socioeconomic status, and even though this same category includes persons who describe themselves as 'retired', it was felt that an older person who said he was 'retired' rather than a 'pensioner' would also differ in socioeconomic status. The fact that this category turned out to be closely related to the socioeconomic status component suggests that this decision was probably correct. On the other hand, the owner-occupancy ratio, which also was included in the socioeconomic status section, might have been better considered with these demographic variables, as Table 3.3 shows it to be more closely related to the zone in transition component than to socioeconomic status.

Table 4.1 presents a similar series of statistics to those discussed in the preceding chapter. Again the variation from one residential area

E

TABLE 4.1 Some statistics relating to the distribution of 24 household and demographic characteristics over 611 ACDs, Melbourne, 1961

(1) Characteristic	(2) First quartile	(3) Median	(4) Third quartile	(5) IQR	(6) Unweighted	(7) Standard deviation	(8) Coefficient of concentration
1 % private houses	94·6	89·4	79·7	14·9	83·8	16·6	0·59
2 % shared private houses	6·4	4·0	2·1	4·3	4·6	3·2	0·40
3 % flats	8·6	3·4	1·6	7·0	7·9	11·6	0·68
4 % rooms and apartments	2·2	0·6	0·1	2·1	2·4	5·0	0·79
5 % non-private dwellings	1·5	0·5	0·2	1·3	1·1	1·6	0·67
6 % population change, 1954-61	177	108	98	79	174	199	n. app.[a]
7 Persons per sq. mile	11,390	7,826	4,736	6,654	8,661	5,803	n. app.
8 Adults per dwelling	3·0	2·8	2·6	0·4	2·8	0·4	n. app.
9 Fertility ratio	589	426	352	237	466	155	n. app.
10 % population 0-14	35·0	26·0	21·4	13·6	28·0	8·2	0·23
11 % population 15-24	15·8	14·5	12·8	3·0	14·3	2·4	0·11
12 % population 25-44	31·6	28·1	24·8	6·8	28·3	4·6	0·13
13 % population 45-64	25·4	21·8	15·5	9·9	20·7	6·0	0·21
14 % population 65 and over	12·2	8·8	4·6	7·6	8·7	4·5	0·33
15 % males in workforce	66·5	61·9	57·6	8·9	62·0	6·0	0·14
16 % females in workforce	29·2	24·5	19·7	9·5	25·2	7·2	0·21
17 Dependency ratio	160	134	111	49	134	32	n. app.
18 % pensioners	8·4	6·4	3·7	4·7	6·1	2·8	0·28
19 % adult women in home duties	57·7	51·0	43·3	14·4	50·2	9·6	0·21
20 % population male	51·1	49·9	48·5	2·6	49·6	3·1	0·05
21 % never-married adults	22·0	18·7	12·9	9·1	18·1	6·3	0·21
22 % permanently separated	1·9	1·3	0·9	1·0	1·6	1·2	0·34
23 % widowed	7·1	5·4	3·1	4·0	5·2	2·3	0·27
24 % divorced	1·0	0·6	0·4	0·6	0·8	0·6	0·39

[a] n. app. = not applicable.

to another is in many cases quite marked. For example, although the mean percentage of private houses in all 611 areas was 84 per cent, in one area in four the percentage was 95 per cent or greater. By comparing columns 3 and 6 we can also see that there were many areas with quite low proportions of private houses, and in thirty-two areas fewer than half the occupied dwellings were private houses. Most of these areas were located, as might be expected, in the inner-city district, where flats, rooms, apartments, and non-private accommodation predominate. There was also considerable variation in population density, and although Melbourne, like other Australian cities, is characterised by an overall low level of population density, in the inner city areas residential densities of 20,000 persons to the square mile or higher are not uncommon.

As Table 4.1 suggests, the distributions by dwelling type were much more concentrated than the various demographic categories considered. While indexes of residential concentration cannot be calculated for some ratios, the first five far exceed those for the remaining variables. For example, only in three areas in Melbourne did the proportion of children under fifteen fall below 10 per cent of the population, and in half the areas it varied between 21 and 35 per cent. By comparison, there were thirty-five areas where more than 10 per cent of the occupied dwellings consisted of rooms or apartments, and forty-seven areas where at least 25 per cent of the dwellings were flats. But of course even in areas where rooms and flats predominate dependent children are found, and it is because the type of available housing does not rule out this possibility that the demographic characteristics show a lower degree of spatial concentration than the dwelling variables. It is interesting, however, that the aged, pensioners, widowed, separated, and divorced are more highly concentrated in their residential distribution than the other demographic categories, a finding which reflects the tendency for persons having these characteristics to reside in, or gravitate towards, inner city areas. Maps showing the location of these groups indicate quite clearly that they are heavily overrepresented in what Burgess designated the zone in transition and what Shevky and Bell named the areas of high urbanisation. In Melbourne these areas are concentrated mainly south of the city centre, in Albert Park, South Yarra, Prahran, and St Kilda, and to a lesser extent Brighton. These are the areas of the flat-dwellers, of high mobility and economic activity, where most of the adult population, including women, are engaged in full-time work. Interestingly enough, of all seventy variables analysed in this monograph the workforce participation and dependency ratios were the most highly centralised in their residential distribution. The further any area was from the CBD, the lower its male and female workforce participation rates tended to be ($r = -0·64$ and $-0·71$ respectively). Likewise the ratio of dependants to workers tended to rise as one moved from the inner city into the suburbs ($r = 0·72$). No other demographic, socioeconomic, or ethnic characteristics showed such high degrees of centralisation, although most showed some tendency to increase or decline with increasing distance.

Because so many of these demographic and household characteristics are closely related (areas with high percentages of private houses or children under fifteen are almost bound to have relatively few flats or old people), it is not surprising that the residential distributions of most of these characteristics overlap considerably. Table 4.2 presents the simple correlations between all pairs of characteristics.

Taking the first characteristic as an example, we see that areas with high percentages of private houses tend to have low percentages of shared houses, flats, rooms and apartments, and non-private dwellings, to have experienced relatively greater population growth during the intercensal period 1954-61, to be of lower population density and have fewer adults per dwelling, to have relatively high fertility ratios, younger populations, lower workforce participation rates and higher dependency ratios, and few pensioners, unmarried adults, separated, widowed, or divorced persons. And so we could go on. The general picture that emerges is a familiar one, and as one examines the pattern of correlations shown in Table 4.2, the city almost seems to divide itself naturally into areas with quite dissimilar household characteristics. The inner city districts, with their mixed populations of older persons approaching the end of the life cycle, young unmarried adults seeking flats and rooms close to work and the bright lights, and social isolates seeking perhaps the anonymity of the inner city, readily distinguish themselves from the working class districts immediately surrounding them and from the home-and-garden syndrome of life in the dormitory suburbs further out.

As in the preceding chapter, the technique of component analysis has been used to extract from Table 4.2 generalised measures of underlying dimensions of residential differentiation. The results of this analysis are shown in Table 4.3 and again indicate the usefulness of the Shevky scheme.

The first component, identified as household composition, explains 60 per cent of the original variance among these twenty-four measures. It is six times more important than the next largest component, a difference which reflects the high and systematic intercorrelations among

	1	2	3	4	5	6	7	8	9	10	11	12	13	14	15	16	17	18	19	20	21	22	23	24
1 % private houses	100	-59	-89	-78	-68	44	-44	-54	67	78	-55	29	-57	-62	-70	-80	73	-53	76	16	-77	-74	-66	-79
2 % shared private houses		100	39	49	50	-39	31	47	-42	-50	41	-23	43	48	51	51	-58	50	-47	-03	50	45	50	46
3 % flats			100	63	52	-41	34	30	-66	-70	45	-42	60	63	52	65	-55	51	-65	-24	69	61	66	71
4 % rooms and apartments				100	72	-31	51	62	-57	-68	49	-23	48	55	64	75	-68	52	-72	-11	71	74	60	73
5 % non-private dwellings					100	-29	50	64	-48	-65	51	-15	43	52	67	75	-73	50	-73	-03	72	75	56	72
6 % population change, 1954-61						100	-23	-25	59	52	-35	37	-65	-63	-44	-36	45	-59	37	09	-50	-32	-59	-41
7 Persons per sq. mile							100	51	-48	-49	32	-11	39	34	60	65	-63	46	-55	07	54	59	47	53
8 Adults per dwelling								100	-45	-50	55	-09	32	29	59	66	-65	34	-58	10	62	57	35	49
9 Fertility ratio									100	85	-69	66	-87	-75	-68	-74	71	-66	69	22	-86	-54	-79	-66
10 % population 0-14										100	-64	56	-87	-85	-85	-82	81	-74	76	19	-90	-66	-89	-80
11 % population 15-24											100	-53	57	47	60	68	-68	47	-62	-09	77	52	50	50
12 % population 25-44												100	-78	-73	-19	-24	19	-65	35	28	-60	-20	-68	-32
13 % population 45-64													100	91	65	58	-61	82	-58	-22	81	48	90	64
14 % population 65 and over														100	58	53	-53	89	-59	-25	77	51	94	67
15 % males in workforce															100	86	-95	57	-72	-03	76	72	66	74
16 % females in workforce																100	-95	52	-86	-06	84	81	64	80
17 Dependency ratio																	100	-56	78	00	-79	-78	-64	-76
18 % pensioners																		100	-60	-15	70	61	86	65
19 % adult women in home duties																			100	49	-75	-84	-59	-83
20 % population male																				100	-03	-16	-07	-25
21 % never-married adults																					100	68	84	75
22 % permanently separated																						100	56	81
23 % widowed																							100	71
24 % divorced																								100

TABLE 4.3   Factor coefficients between 24 household and demographic characteristics and three principal components (unities in the principal diagonal of correlation matrix)

Primary variable	Factor coefficients for components		
	Household composition	Second component	Sex composition
1 % private houses	0·85	–0·16	0·18
2 % shared private houses	–0·60	0·09	0·15
3 % flats	–0·76	–0·08	–0·30
4 % rooms and apartments	–0·79	0·28	–0·12
5 % non-private dwellings	–0·76	0·36	–0·02
6 % population change, 1954-61	0·57	0·35	–0·21
7 Persons per sq. mile	–0·61	0·32	0·18
8 Adults per dwelling	–0·63	0·46	0·22
9 Fertility ratio	0·86	0·27	–0·05
10 % population 0-14	0·94	0·14	–0·02
11 % population 15-24	–0·71	0·00	0·12
12 % population 25-44	0·52	0·72	–0·02
13 % population 45-64	–0·83	–0·49	0·12
14 % population 65 and over	–0·82	–0·48	0·03
15 % males in workforce	–0·85	0·24	0·14
16 % females in workforce	–0·89	0·34	–0·01
17 Dependency ratio	0·87	–0·32	–0·14
18 % pensioners	–0·79	–0·36	0·12
19 % adult women in home duties	0·87	–0·18	0·38
20 % population male	0·19	0·29	0·84
21 % never-married adults	–0·93	–0·06	0·14
22 % permanently separated	–0·81	0·33	–0·18
23 % widowed	–0·86	–0·36	0·16
24 % divorced	–0·87	0·12	–0·23
Eigenvalue (V_p)	14·42	2·56	1·35
100 V_p/24	60·08	10·67	5·63

the measures included in this section. The pattern of factor coefficients indicates that this component discriminates the life style and family composition of the suburbs from that of the inner city, and although I have usually preferred the more neutral term 'household composition' in identifying this component, I will use the term 'familism' interchangeably with it. This usage has the important advantage that it is simpler to talk about areas with 'high familism' or 'low familism', and it avoids the necessity to repeat in detail the differentiating characteristics of 'household composition' as measured by this particular scale. However, it is emphasised that when areas are described as having 'high familism' the term is applied in a restricted sense, to describe areas characterised by relatively many private houses and young children, high fertility and dependency ratios, low workforce participation rates, and few old people or unmarried adults. By 'low familism' the opposite to this is meant, without any subjective, behavioural, or evaluative overtones. The extent to which these aggregate, residential differences in modes of household arrangement are systematically associated with individual differences in family life, behaviour, and attitudes is a matter that can be established directly only by further examination. There is considerable evidence that such differences can be identified (Bell 1965), but this is not a point on which direct evidence for Australia is readily available (Martin 1967; Elkin 1957).

It will be noted that the second component shown on Table 4.3 has not been given a meaning. This is because it is difficult to interpret. Its highest positive weights are for the percentage of persons aged 25-44 years and the number of adults per dwelling, its highest negative ones for the percentage of persons aged 45-64 years, and 65 years of age and older. This indicates that subsidiary age differentials among adults can be identified independently of the first component, but beyond this it is difficult to say more. It is of some interest that when component scores for the 611 ACDs were computed for this component they correlated negatively with the socioeconomic status scores derived in the preceding chapter ($r = -0 \cdot 70$). This suggests that this second component is in effect attempting to measure differences in socioeconomic status to the extent that they are reflected in household and demographic characteristics. It further implies that the measures shown in Table 4.3 are not strictly unidimensional, a conclusion applicable to several measures in the socioeconomic status chapter as well. If these potential measures *were* unidimensional, the first component would explain virtually all the variance among the measures and not simply a very much larger proportion than any other component.

The third component, unlike the second, has a relatively direct interpretation, with by far its highest loading on the twentieth variable. It distinguishes areas with high masculinity from areas of low masculinity. It is interesting that this emerges as an independent factor from the analysis, but as it and the second component jointly account for only one-sixth of the variance we shall not pursue them in the following discussion.

A series of familism scores was computed, using the weights shown in the first column of Table 4.3. These scores are mapped on Fig. 4, in five groups consisting of equal numbers of areas ranging from high to low familism. As this map shows, familism conforms very closely to the classic zonal scheme, with areas of low familism being located near the central

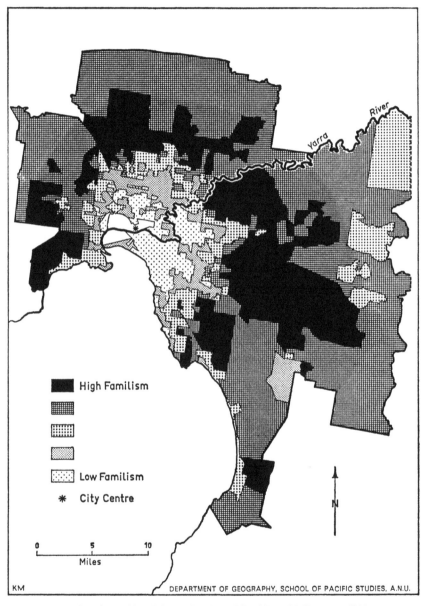

FIG. 4   The residential distribution of familism, Melbourne, 1961

Key to Fig. 4

First quintile group (high familism)

25	58	91	260	325	369	390	462	542	567
27	59	95	271	326	370	391	464	543	568
28	60	96	273	327	371	392	466	544	573
30	61	165	279	328	372	401	467	545	576
31	62	167	282	334	374	432	474	546	577
34	63	190	284	335	375	433	475	547	578
50	64	191	287	336	377	434	518	548	579
51	65	254	317	337	378	435	519	549	580
52	66	255	318	341	379	437	536	550	583
53	67	257	319	345	380	443	537	561	594
54	68	258	320	351	382	445	538	562	597
55	89	259	324	352	385	460	541	563	611
57	90								

Second quintile group

23	150	256	311	373	424	495	526	571	592
24	166	264	312	381	436	496	527	572	593
26	168	266	322	383	438	497	528	574	595
49	172	272	323	384	446	498	529	575	596
56	184	274	333	386	448	499	530	581	598
69	187	275	340	387	461	500	533	582	602
97	188	276	342	388	463	517	539	584	603
114	201	278	343	389	465	520	540	585	604
119	219	280	344	393	473	521	551	586	605
123	235	281	346	397	492	522	566	587	607
145	238	285	354	398	493	523	569	588	609
146	251	286	368	400	494	524	570	591	610
149	253								

Third quintile group

11	70	117	158	222	268	338	425	472	557
21	84	118	159	223	283	339	427	477	558
22	92	126	162	228	296	347	430	478	559
29	98	127	164	233	297	349	431	480	564
32	99	129	169	234	310	350	439	525	565
33	100	144	171	236	315	353	440	531	589
35	105	147	173	237	316	355	441	532	590
36	106	148	186	252	321	357	442	534	599
39	110	153	192	261	329	376	444	535	600
44	111	154	193	262	330	396	447	552	601
45	112	155	199	263	331	399	469	553	606
47	113	156	206	267	332	423	470	556	608
48	115	157							

Key to Fig. 4—*continued*

Fourth quintile group

6	74	94	133	179	204	232	306	364	449
8	76	101	135	181	205	243	307	365	450
9	77	104	136	182	211	265	313	366	452
10	78	108	138	183	212	269	314	367	456
12	80	109	141	185	214	270	348	394	457
13	81	116	152	189	215	277	356	395	471
16	82	121	160	194	220	289	358	402	476
37	83	122	161	195	224	290	359	403	479
41	85	124	163	197	225	298	360	405	486
42	86	125	170	200	227	299	361	426	554
46	87	128	176	202	229	302	362	428	555
72	88	131	177	203	230	305	363	429	560
73	93								

Fifth quintile group (low familism)

1	40	139	208	241	293	408	420	483	505
2	43	140	209	242	294	409	421	484	506
3	71	142	210	244	295	410	422	485	507
4	75	143	213	245	300	411	451	487	508
5	79	151	216	246	301	412	453	488	509
7	102	174	217	247	303	413	454	489	510
14	103	175	218	248	304	414	455	490	511
15	107	178	221	249	308	415	458	491	512
17	120	180	226	250	309	416	459	501	513
18	130	196	231	288	404	417	468	502	514
19	132	198	239	291	406	418	481	503	515
20	134	207	240	292	407	419	482	504	516
38	137								

city. With increasing distance the level of familism rises, reaching its peak in areas eight to ten miles from the CBD. The correlation between distance from the city centre and these familism scores was very much higher than was the case with the socioeconomic status scores ($r = 0 \cdot 60$ and $0 \cdot 32$ respectively), supporting the suggestion that in the case of socioeconomic status sectoral differences were more marked than zonal differences. It can be suggested, indeed, that Hoyt's sectoral scheme is generally more applicable to the analysis of the areal distribution of socioeconomic status, whereas Burgess's zonal scheme applies more widely to household and demographic characteristics. However, even in the case of the familism scores, areas on the perimeter of the metropolis usually displayed somewhat lower familism than those slightly less distant. This reflects the pattern of metropolitan growth and the extension of suburbia into exurbia, with the gradual incorporation of older extra-metropolitan settlements. This process is well illustrated by growth east of the city towards the Dandenong hills, where numerous established settlements have gradually been absorbed into the metropolitan area. But it can also be seen on the northern, western, and southern fringes of the metropolis. Some of these areas were, and still are, popular places for retirement and week-end retreats.

The broad differences between areas with differing levels of 'familism' can be illustrated by presenting abridged profiles of seven areas, selected as before from the middle of each of the five groups. The areas with the highest and lowest scores on the familism scale are also shown. The five characteristics selected represent some of the more important measures included in the scale.

Again the differences between areas are marked and systematic. The first area grew from only 146 persons in 1954 to 3,167 by 1961, the second highest rate of population growth in the whole of Melbourne

TABLE 4.4   Abridged familism profiles of seven residential areas, Melbourne, 1961

Area	% private houses	% population 0-14	% females in workforce	% never-married adults	% widowed, separated or divorced
568 (high familism)	100	51	15	8	2
460	98	37	16	10	6
119	96	29	16	16	5
158	93	27	27	18	7
94	82	23	27	25	9
509	55	19	34	23	12
481 (low familism)	2	5	55	51	13

during this intercensal period. It had the third highest percentage of children under fifteen and the fourth highest percentage of private houses of any area in the city. But as the map and Table 4.4 suggest, there were many other newly developed parts of the city the demographic characteristics of which were not so very different. In almost all the 122 areas with the highest familism scores, well over one-third of the population was under fifteen years of age, and the percentage of private houses exceeded 95 per cent of all dwellings (cf. Table 4.1). At the other end of the scale came a central city district immediately south of the 'Golden Mile'—the area bounded by St Kilda and Queen's Roads. This, with areas nearby to the east and south, represents a typical area of high urbanisation, consisting almost entirely of flats (90 per cent), rooms and apartments (3 per cent), and non-private dwellings (3 per cent). Its population, which declined very slightly over the intercensal period from 1,729 to 1,522 persons, consisted in 1961 largely of single, working adults: 88 per cent of males were at work, and among females 55 per cent. These figures can be compared with the overall metropolitan averages of 62 and 25 per cent respectively. As Fig. 4 shows, areas with similar characteristics formed a relatively continuous belt north, east, and south of the city centre, from Parkville through parts of Carlton, Fitzroy, East Melbourne, Richmond, South Yarra, Prahran, Windsor, St Kilda, Albert Park, and South Melbourne. Since 1961 these areas have no doubt been further extended, partly through planned redevelopment and partly because of unplanned processes of ecological succession and changing land use.

A final question that can be asked in this section is what relationship, if any, existed between the socioeconomic level of an area and its level of familism. Is there any systematic relationship between these two dimensions of residential differentiation? The answer to this question is a definite 'No'. There is no correlation between these scales, and the socioeconomic status scores derived in Chapter 3 have virtually a zero correlation with scores on familism ($r = + 0.04$). This means that areas with high socioeconomic status differed as much in their level of familism as areas with low socioeconomic status. To put it another way, the accuracy of any prediction about the level of familism in a given area would not be improved by knowing its socioeconomic status score. For example, the area with the lowest level of familism (ACD 481) ranked relatively high in socioeconomic status (61st out of 611), whereas the area with the second lowest level of familism (ACD 218) ranked very low on socioeconomic status (554th). At the 'high familism' end of the scale, the area with the highest level of familism had low socioeconomic status but other areas with almost equally high levels of familism had relatively high socioeconomic status. In this study the dimensions of socioeconomic status and familism are independent empirically as well as analytically.

This finding, that there is no overall relationship at the aggregate, residential level between the socioeconomic status of an area and its degree of familism, is both interesting and surprising. Does it mean that at the individual level there is also no relationship between socioeconomic status and fertility? We have stressed throughout that ecological data of the kind analysed in this monograph cannot properly answer questions about individuals. Nonetheless, if social class differences in family size were considerable in Australia—and there is no contemporary evidence at all about such differentials—it would be reasonable to expect that areas with high socioeconomic status would tend to have fewer children under fifteen and lower fertility ratios than areas with low socioeconomic status. That no such difference emerges at the ecological level suggests that differentials in fertility by social class in contemporary Australia may not be particularly marked. Alternatively our measurements may not be sufficiently discriminating to identify their effects. But these can only be suggestions, and firm answers wait upon future research.

The fact that the socioeconomic status and familism scores are empirically independent means that they provide a highly efficient pair of axes for classifying residential areas in Melbourne, as the information contained in them does not overlap at all. However, before attempting to develop such a classification we have to consider the third major dimension of residential differentiation—religious persuasion and ethnic origin.

5

Ethnic and Religious Composition

Since the end of World War II, Melbourne's population has increased by over 50 per cent, from one and a quarter millions in 1947 to almost two millions by 1961. Of this increase approximately half was due directly to the arrival of overseas-born settlers, many of whom came from countries little represented in the migration of earlier periods. In 1947 Melbourne, like most other parts of Australia, had a relatively homogeneous population, with 98 per cent of its population born in Australia, New Zealand, or the United Kingdom. Admittedly some of these Australian-born persons were descended from the German, Scandinavian, Italian, and Chinese immigrants of earlier years, but even so it is still true that in 1947 the bulk of the Australian population was British in descent, culture, and identification. To many the United Kingdom was, and still is, the 'Mother Country'.

By 1961 this picture had changed substantially—how substantially can be gauged from Table 5.1, which depicts the main shifts in ethnic composition in the post-war period. According to these figures the most dramatic decline occurred in the relative position of the native-born, whose share of the total population fell from 90 per cent at the end of the

TABLE 5.1   Changes in the ethnic composition of Melbourne, 1947-61

Birthplace	1947	Percentage 1954	1961
Australia	89·8	82·8	76·7
New Zealand	0·7	0·6	0·5
United Kingdom	7·2	8·0	8·1
Germany	0·3	0·9	1·5
Greece	0·2	0·4	1·5
Italy	0·4	2·0	3·9
Malta	0·0	0·4	0·9
Netherlands	0·0	0·5	1·1
Poland	0·1	1·1	1·1
Other countries	1·4	3·4	4·7
Total	100·1	100·1	100·0
Number (000's)	1,226	1,524	1,912

war to 77 per cent in 1961. This decline does not reflect any major increase in the proportion of British settlers, but is due rather to increases in migration from southern Europe and, to a lesser degree, from northern, central, and eastern Europe as well. In 1947 Melbourne's settlers from Italy, Greece, or Malta amounted to less than 0·5 per cent of the total population, a figure that had increased tenfold by 1961, to over 5 per cent. In some parts of the city this figure rose to well over one-third. In the municipality of Fitzroy, for example, 32 per cent of the population were born in one of these three countries. Among other birthplace groups the rate of growth has been even more rapid. Over the same period the Dutch increased from 1 in 2,500 to 1 in 90 of the total population. In fact all the major non-British groups listed in Table 5.1 showed rapid rates of growth over this fourteen-year period. Perhaps an even more graphic sense of the magnitude of these changes can be conveyed by quoting the absolute numbers involved. In 1947 only 28,000 of Melbourne's population had been born in countries other than Australia, New Zealand, or the United Kingdom. By 1961 this figure had risen to 280,000, a tenfold increase during a period when total population grew by only 50 per cent.

Changes in ethnic composition can have an important impact on the religious composition of a country. As Price (1957) has shown for the period 1947 to 1954, increasing migration from continental Europe added significantly to the relative strength of the Roman Catholic, Orthodox, and Lutheran denominations, mainly because the proportion of new arrivals with these religious affiliations far exceeded their proportion in Australia's resident population at the end of the war. The net effect of changes in the ethnic origins of Melbourne's post-war settlers on the religious composition of the city can be seen from Table 5.2. This table shows very clearly the relative decline among the major Protestant denominations—Church of England, Presbyterian, and Methodist—from 60 per cent of the total at the end of the war to 49 per cent by the early 1960s, the relative stability of the smaller Protestant groups (except for the Lutherans, who increased rapidly over the period), and the substantial increases among adherents of the Catholic and Orthodox (mainly Greek Orthodox) churches. This Orthodox figure embraces the members of all Orthodox churches (Price 1957), including Bulgarian Eastern Orthodox, Czech Orthodox, Russian Orthodox, Serbian Orthodox, and Greek Orthodox, to name only a few. Of course part of the increase in the Catholic percentage has to be attributed to the higher rate of natural increase among Catholics than Protestants (Day 1965), and not only to migration. But their total

TABLE 5.2   Changes in the religious composition of Melbourne, 1947-61

Religion		Percentage	
	1947	1954	1961
Baptist	1·8	1·6	1·4
Brethren	0·1	0·2	0·1
Catholic	20·9	23·5	27·1
Church of Christ	1·6	1·5	1·4
Church of England	37·2	35·4	31·0
Congregational	0·7	0·6	0·5
Orthodox	n.a.[a]	1·0	2·5
Lutheran	0·1	0·6	1·0
Methodist	9·9	8·8	7·8
Presbyterian	11·8	11·1	10·3
Salvation Army	0·6	0·5	0·5
Seventh Day Adventist	0·1	0·1	0·2
Hebrew[b]	1·2	1·5	1·5
Other[c]	2·6	2·8	2·8
No religion	0·5	0·3	0·5
No reply	10·9	10·6	11·5
Total	100·0	100·1	100·1

[a] n.a. = not available. A small number (0·2 per cent), who described themselves as 'Greek Catholics', were included in the 'Catholic' category.
[b] 'Hebrew' is the term used in the census classification. The term 'Jewish' is used interchangeably in the text.
[c] Including Protestant (undefined), other Christian, other non-Christian, and indefinite.

growth is too great to be explained in terms of differential fertility alone.

Obviously the relationship between ethnic origin and religious affiliation is close, and it is for this reason that I have extended the concept of segregation (ethnic status) to include religious differences as well. Such an extension would not have been possible in comparable studies in the United States, as religion is not asked on their census schedule. In Australia it is an optional question, hence the large percentage of Australians who give no reply. This should not be equated with the 'no religion' category, which is very small. In field surveys where a question on religion is asked without suggesting that it is optional, it usually happens that the majority of those who give no reply in the census in fact offer a religious affiliation. In a recent survey of social stratification in Australia the non-response rate to a question on religious affiliation was only 0·4 per cent, but the 'no religion' category accounted for only 2·7 per cent of respondents. Clearly the majority of those giving no reply in the census are simply exercising their right of non-response.

TABLE 5.3 The religious composition of selected birthplace categories, Melbourne, 1961
(percentages)

Religion	Aust.	New Zealand	United Kingdom	Germany	Greece	Italy	Malta	Nether-lands	Poland	Other Europe	Other World	Total	No. (000's)
Baptist	87·1	0·5	8·8	0·2	*	0·2	*	0·9	0·1	0·7	1·4	99·9	27
Brethren	78·2	1·2	16·9	0·1	*	0·3	*	1·5	*	0·4	1·4	100·0	3
Catholic	68·1	0·3	3·6	1·7	*	13·0	3·0	1·9	1·7	5·0	1·7	100·0	518
Church of Christ	94·7	0·4	3·5	0·2	*	0·1	*	0·1	*	0·2	0·8	100·0	26
Church of England	85·1	0·6	12·9	0·2	*	*	*	0·1	*	0·3	0·9	100·1	593
Congregational	88·2	0·6	9·8	0·2	*	0·1	*	0·2	*	0·1	0·8	100·0	9
Orthodox	20·3	*	0·1	1·2	52·7	0·2	*	*	1·2	11·9	12·3	99·9	49
Lutheran	22·6	*	0·3	40·3	*	0·1	*	0·6	1·1	33·8	1·3	100·1	19
Methodist	92·4	0·4	5·8	0·1	*	*	*	0·2	*	0·2	0·8	99·9	149
Presbyterian	86·3	0·7	10·2	0·2	*	*	*	1·3	*	0·5	0·8	100·0	196
Salvation Army	88·7	0·7	9·4	0·1	*	0·1	*	0·4	*	0·3	0·4	100·1	5
Seventh Day Adventist	79·2	2·4	6·6	1·2	*	0·1	*	0·7	0·3	6·0	3·4	99·9	3
Hebrew	36·9	0·4	6·7	6·5	*	0·2	*	0·3	26·2	17·0	5·7	99·9	29
Other	65·7	0·6	10·7	7·1	0·5	0·8	0·1	3·5	0·5	5·3	5·2	100·0	54
No religion	65·0	1·3	11·8	3·4	0·2	0·7	0·1	10·4	0·6	2·8	3·8	100·1	9
No reply	76·7	0·5	7·7	2·0	1·2	2·5	0·4	2·3	1·2	3·4	2·0	99·9	219
Total	76·7	0·5	8·1	1·5	1·5	3·9	0·9	1·1	1·1	3·0	1·7	100·0	1,912

* = less than 0·1 per cent.

F

A more direct way of looking at the relationship between religion and ethnic origin is to examine the birthplace composition of different religious groups. This is done in Table 5.3. If there were no relationship between these two characteristics, then we should expect to find that all the figures in this table would be the same as those shown along the bottom row: for each religious category, we would find that 77 per cent were Australian-born, 0·5 per cent born in New Zealand, 8 per cent in the United Kingdom, and so on. But it can readily be seen that this expectation is not realised. Some religious groups have far above the expected percentages, and others are well below. The most Australian religious categories are Church of Christ and Methodist, followed by the Salvation Army, Baptist, and Presbyterian. The most immigrant are the Orthodox, Lutheran, and Jewish churches, all of which consist predominantly of overseas-born persons. An inspection of the rows of this table also reveals some interesting relationships, for example, the relative over-representation of New Zealanders in the Brethren and Seventh Day Adventist groups (and also 'no religion' category). But these are small groups, and obviously most New Zealanders are Anglicans, Presbyterians, or Catholics.

Equally important as such differences between ethnic groups is the high degree of religious homogeneity among the southern European groups compared with northwestern European settlers. Thus, whereas almost all Greek-born persons identified themselves as Greek Orthodox and almost all the Italian-born and Maltese-born were Catholics, Germans were evenly divided between the Catholic and Lutheran churches, with a smaller number identifying as Jews. The Dutch, while mainly a Catholic group, also contained substantial numbers of Protestants. Differences such as these, while interesting in themselves, also become important in interpreting the residential patterns of different ethnic groups, since those with greater religious homogeneity may be reasonably expected to display more marked degrees of residential concentrations than those which are divided among different denominations.

Table 5.4 lists twenty-two ethnic and religious variables from which an ethnicity component can be derived. It will be noticed that not all the religious categories shown on Table 5.3 have been retained, mainly because some were too small for detailed consideration. There were, for example, only about 3,000 Brethren in the whole city, or 0·1 per cent of the total population. Thus, in any one area one would expect to find on average only five persons belonging to that religious group. This amounts to only a little more than one household, so that it becomes difficult if not impossible to make meaningful generalisations about the residential distribution of such a small group. Throughout this study I have in fact restricted my analysis to census categories which account for at least 1 per cent of the total population of Melbourne as a whole.

The birthplace categories comprise all those for which information by CDs is available, but only the total number of persons of alien nationality is considered. Separate information on the number of Dutch, German, Greek, Italian, Polish, and Yugoslav nationals is also available, but as this did not seem to add significantly to the birthplace data it has not been included. Similarly, a relatively wide range of information on length of residence in Australia was analysed, but again only data for those in Australia for more than one year but less than four years have been presented here. Because of the high proportion of temporary visitors included in the less-than-one-year category, they were excluded from analysis. Since foreign-born persons of non-British nationality must fulfil a five-year residence qualification before they can become naturalised, there is obviously bound to be a high correlation between the percentage of aliens in an area and the percentage of foreign-born persons with less than four years' residence in Australia.

The statistics shown on Table 5.4 indicate quite clearly that the variation in these ethnic and religious characteristics from one area to another was very considerable—more marked in fact than for socio-economic or demographic characteristics. There were many characteristics which displayed relatively high degrees of residential concentration—the Orthodox, Jews, Greeks, Italians, Maltese, Dutch, and Poles all had coefficients of concentration of 0·5 or greater. If we take the Jews as an example, we can see that although they accounted for 1·5 per cent of Melbourne's population as a whole, in half the 611 areas considered they constituted less than 0·5 per cent of the population (see column 2 of Table 5.4). This means that the Jewish population was heavily concentrated in a small number of areas which had much higher percentages than the average: indeed, in 1961, 75 per cent of Melbourne's Jewish community lived in 100 ACDs which contained only 16 per cent of the total population of the city. In these 100 areas they averaged 7 per cent of the resident population. For the Jews to have had a residential distribution that did not differ from those of other religious faiths, 60 per cent would have needed to move into different areas of residence. For the Maltese a similarly high percentage would have had to re-locate. For other non-British birthplace groups the corresponding figures were: Greeks, 57 per cent; Italians,

TABLE 5.4   Some statistics relating to the distribution of 22 ethnic and religious characteristics of 611 ACDs, Melbourne, 1961

(1) Characteristic	(2) First quartile	(3) Median	(4) Third quartile	(5) IQR	(6) Unweighted mean	(7) Standard deviation	(8) Coefficient of concentration
1 % Baptist	1·9	1·2	0·7	1·2	1·4	1·1	0·40
2 % Catholic	32·1	25·8	19·4	12·7	27·2	9·6	0·27
3 % Church of Christ	1·8	1·2	0·7	1·1	1·4	1·0	0·39
4 % Church of England	35·4	31·7	27·6	7·8	31·1	6·5	0·17
5 % Orthodox	2·9	1·2	0·5	2·4	2·6	3·5	0·62
6 % Lutheran	1·3	0·8	0·5	0·8	1·0	0·7	0·37
7 % Methodist	9·8	7·7	5·6	4·2	7·9	3·1	0·24
8 % Presbyterian	13·3	10·1	7·1	6·2	10·3	4·1	0·25
9 % Hebrew	1·2	0·4	0·1	1·1	1·5	3·4	0·77
10 % no reply	13·2	11·3	9·8	3·4	11·5	2·5	0·14
11 % U.K.	9·3	7·7	5·9	3·4	7·9	2·9	0·21
12 % Germany	1·7	1·1	0·7	1·0	1·5	1·5	0·43
13 % Greece	1·5	0·5	0·1	1·4	1·5	2·7	0·73
14 % Italy	4·9	1·9	0·7	4·2	3·9	5·3	0·64
15 % Malta	1·0	0·2	0·0	1·0	0·9	1·8	0·77
16 % Netherlands	1·1	0·6	0·3	0·8	1·1	1·5	0·60
17 % Poland	1·2	0·6	0·3	0·9	1·1	1·5	0·59
18 % other Europe	3·7	2·3	1·4	2·3	2·9	2·4	0·41
19 % other World	2·2	1·5	1·0	1·2	1·7	1·0	0·31
20 % Australia	84·3	79·0	71·3	13·0	77·0	9·9	0·30
21 % residence 1-3 years	5·4	3·2	1·9	3·5	3·9	2·5	0·38
22 % aliens	11·7	7·0	3·1	8·6	8·5	7·2	0·48

50 per cent; Dutch, 46 per cent; Poles, 45 per cent; and Germans, 31 per cent.

Similarly, a comparison of columns 3 and 6 of Table 5.4 suggests considerable diversity in the areal distribution of these ethnic and religious characteristics. Among the most concentrated groups, the unweighted mean is much higher than the median, indicating a distribution skewed markedly towards higher values. Thus there are seventy areas where Italians account for 10 per cent or more of the total population, a figure two and a half times greater than the metropolitan average.

Detailed maps showing the location of each religious and ethnic group have been prepared, but are not reproduced here for reasons of space. Many groups showed highly centralised distributions, that for the Greek-born being the highest ($r = -0\cdot65$). The further an area was from the central city, the smaller its Greek population tended to be. In fact all the foreign birthplace categories were concentrated in the inner suburbs except the Dutch and the British, whose relative numbers tended to increase with distance from the CBD ($r = 0\cdot45$ and $0\cdot46$ respectively). The German-born were divided between the inner and outer suburbs (the correlation between distance from the CBD and percentage German-born being virtually zero, $r = -0\cdot05$), but this probably reflects the fact that this group is internally heterogeneous. It consists partly of German ethnics but also of children born to displaced persons in camps in Germany during and after the war. Although a detailed crosstabulation of birthplace by nationality is not available for 1954 or 1961, Zubrzycki's work on the records of the International Refugee Organization indicates that perhaps half Australia's net permanent intake of 54,039 German-born persons between 1947 and 1954 consisted of nationals of countries other than Germany—mainly Poland, the Ukraine, Yugoslavia, and the Baltic countries (Zubrzycki 1960:51-7).

From the preceding discussion the reader will have inferred that some ethnic groups live in the same parts of the metropolis. Table 5.5 measures the degree of association among the residential distributions of these various characteristics in a more precise way. For illustrative purposes let us take one of the religious categories with a moderately concentrated residential distribution—the Lutherans (column 6 and row 6). The residential distribution of the members of this denomination was virtually uncorrelated with those of the first three groups and showed slight correlations with the next three. In fact the residential distribution of this group did not seem to follow that of many other groups, and only two of its correlation coefficients

TABLE 5.5 Intercorrelations between the residential distributions of 22 ethnic and religious characteristics

	1	2	3	4	5	6	7	8	9	10	11	12	13	14	15	16	17	18	19	20	21	22
1 % Baptist	100	-35	27	28	-27	06	49	41	-14	-24	15	-16	-30	-20	-25	01	-20	-23	-28	39	-31	-33
2 % Catholic		100	-37	-84	65	05	-61	-76	-14	27	-50	17	62	76	75	-22	33	41	22	-63	48	69
3 % Church of Christ			100	35	-34	00	52	36	-14	-17	09	-23	-37	-18	-30	10	-38	-39	-31	46	-34	-35
4 % Church of England				100	-67	-16	56	66	05	-21	50	-32	-63	-72	-65	14	-44	-56	-33	74	-59	-77
5 % Orthodox					100	19	-52	-62	06	17	-40	29	87	68	58	-20	50	62	44	-66	59	75
6 % Lutheran						100	-11	-01	-04	09	26	67	06	16	14	39	32	56	21	-38	37	37
7 % Methodist							100	59	-12	-31	21	-35	-52	-42	-48	06	-43	-53	-40	70	-53	-60
8 % Presbyterian								100	10	-46	45	-10	-60	-60	-63	23	-25	-36	-21	62	-48	-64
9 % Hebrew									100	-35	-13	05	16	-01	-28	-21	38	26	45	-03	02	01
10 % no reply										100	13	16	18	17	39	14	01	09	-07	-30	26	30
11 % U.K.											100	27	-42	-48	-29	52	-11	-09	-10	04	05	-26
12 % Germany												100	18	17	22	45	59	69	33	-61	57	51
13 % Greece													100	66	51	-28	44	54	39	-61	55	70
14 % Italy														100	60	-19	35	49	21	-63	59	80
15 % Malta															100	-11	30	36	12	-57	42	58
16 % Netherlands																100	-02	07	01	-17	25	11
17 % Poland																	100	75	42	-58	45	52
18 % other Europe																		100	49	-75	67	72
19 % other World																			100	-47	41	40
20 % Australia																				100	-89	-91
21 % residence 1-3 years																					100	87
22 % aliens																						100

exceeded 0·5—with percentage born in Germany and percentage born in parts of Europe other than those specified on Table 5.5. It showed lower correlations with percentage born in the Netherlands (positive), with percentage Australian-born (negative), with recent immigrants, and with alien nationals (both positive). The fact that areas with relatively more Lutherans tended also to have relatively more Germans and persons from other European countries reflects an individual correlation. As Table 5.3 shows, many persons from these countries were in fact Lutherans. Similarly, the correlations with the last two measures on this table reflect individual relationships, since many Lutherans are immigrants, some of them recent arrivals from non-British countries. However, the relationship between percentage Lutheran and percentage Dutch is an ecological, or unit, correlation, and reflects a tendency for Dutch persons to live in the same areas as other northwestern European settlers. Very few Lutherans in fact came from Holland (Table 5.3).

If we look at other characteristics, different patterns can be observed. The percentage Jewish, for example, shows only slight correlations with most measures except for the percentages from 'other world' and Poland. Again, these correlations seem to result from individual relationships and reflect the geographical origins of at least part of Melbourne's Jewish population. Other measures, such as the percentage Catholic, Church of England, Presbyterian, and Orthodox, show high interrelationships with several measures, reflecting more systematic and more general patterns of residential association.

In order to identify the main patterns of variation in the residential distributions of these different characteristics, a component analysis was performed on this matrix of correlations, the results of which are given in Table 5.6.

The patterns which emerge from this analysis are very clear indeed, clearer in some respects than those reported in preceding chapters, where one component was difficult to interpret. In this case, all three components have very direct interpretations. The first and most important component, accounting for 43 per cent of the original variance, loads heavily on about half the measures considered. The factor coefficients equal or exceed 0·7 in twelve cases, and the signs of these twelve coefficients indicate that an area with a high score on this component is one with relatively many Catholics, few Anglicans, many Orthodox, few Methodists and Presbyterians, many Greeks, Italians, Maltese, and settlers from other European countries, few Australian-born, and many recently arrived immigrants and alien nationals. Although, therefore, it primarily identifies areas with concentrations

of persons from southern European countries, it also loads on other
more general measures. I have therefore labelled it not 'southern European settlers' but rather 'general ethnic composition'. It does, after all,
have moderate loadings on several other birthplace and religion characteristics as well as those related primarily to southern Europe. The
fact that this first component accounts for three times as much of the
variance as the next largest component again suggests that the framework of analysis we have adopted succeeds in identifying salient dimensions of residential differentiation.

TABLE 5.6   Factor coefficients between 22 ethnic and religious characteristics and three
principal components (unities in the principal diagonal of correlation
matrix)

Primary variable	Factor coefficients for components		
	General ethnic composition	Northwestern European settlers	Areas of Jewish concentration
1 % Baptist	−0·44	0·07	−0·04
2 % Catholic	0·80	−0·39	−0·19
3 % Church of Christ	−0·50	0·00	−0·16
4 % Church of England	−0·84	0·21	0·07
5 % Orthodox	0·83	−0·16	0·11
6 % Lutheran	0·31	0·68	−0·12
7 % Methodist	−0·74	0·02	−0·03
8 % Presbyterian	−0·75	0·38	0·22
9 % Hebrew	0·07	0·11	0·85
10 % no reply	0·32	0·00	−0·63
11 % U.K.	−0·34	0·71	−0·26
12 % Germany	0·51	0·73	−0·04
13 % Greece	0·79	−0·25	0·17
14 % Italy	0·77	−0·27	−0·07
15 % Malta	0·70	−0·25	−0·36
16 % Netherlands	−0·06	0·71	−0·39
17 % Poland	0·63	0·31	0·40
18 % other Europe	0·77	0·40	0·24
19 % other World	0·49	0·23	0·51
20 % Australia	−0·91	−0·26	0·09
21 % residence 1-3 years	0·80	0·33	−0·12
22 % aliens	0·92	0·11	−0·10
Eigenvalue (V_p)	9·43	3·08	2·16
100 $V_p/22$	42·86	14·00	9·82

It is nonetheless very important to notice from Table 5.6 that in
1961 the distribution of Melbourne's ethnic and religious groups
yielded three quite distinct residential patterns. The first, which we
have already discussed, consisted predominantly of southern Euro-

peans, but also other immigrants as well, and was located primarily in the inner-city districts (Fig. 5). The extent to which this ethnic concentration was centralised can be seen from the fact that the correlation between ethnicity and distance from the CBD was -0.63, indicating that areas with high ethnicity (as measured by the first component of Table 5.6) tended to be located near the city centre.

By contrast, the second component identifies a quite distinct pattern of ethnic concentration and has high loadings on the percentages Lutheran, British, German, and Dutch. I have therefore identified this component as 'northwestern European settlers'. The fact that this emerges as a factor uncorrelated with the first and most important component reflects the differential location of these groups in the city. Most of the persons in these categories were located in more distant suburbs. The correlations between distance from the city centre and the percentage born in the United Kingdom or the Netherlands were 0.46 and 0.45 respectively. The third component identifies yet a third pattern of ethnic concentration and differentiates areas with relatively large Jewish populations. These areas tended to be located in middle distance suburbs east and south of the city centre, in suburbs like St Kilda, Elwood, Balaclava, Elsternwick, Caulfield, Hawthorn, and Kew.

What do these results tell us about the usefulness of the framework of analysis which we have adopted for this study? The most important result is that the first component is again very much more important than the lower order components. A single component, identified as general ethnic composition, is able to account for over two-fifths of the original variance among those twenty-two measures of ethnic and religious differentiation. However, the fact that three independent patterns of ethnic distribution can be distinguished also indicates that there are other aspects of residential and social structure not identified by the Shevky formulation. This finding is neither surprising nor discomfiting, since what Shevky and his associates set out to achieve was not to provide an exhaustive analysis of residential differences in modern industrial cities but rather to suggest the most salient and important dimensions along which such differences might be expected to crystallise. Individual cities may well show unique patterns beyond these three basic dimensions. The methods adopted in this monograph enable us to identify what these additional dimensions might be. In cities and countries which do not have marked differences in ethnic and religious composition such a dimension might not emerge at all. In such cases the characteristics of internal (rather than international) migrants could be used to supplement or even replace such an analysis.

Obviously the concept of ethnicity applies only to culturally heterogeneous societies.

The emergence of ethnic concentrations in Melbourne, and for that
matter in other Australian metropolises, is sometimes viewed with concern. But it is a social process that needs to be viewed against the background of the recency of large-scale immigration from non-British
countries, and in the context of cultural and social differences between
the host society and the new settlers. In 1961, 51 per cent of Melbourne's non-British settlers had been in Australia for less than seven
years. Another 35 per cent had arrived some time during the preceding
seven years. General observation suggests that ethnic concentrations
have arisen largely out of the positive, and understandable, desire
among recent immigrants with different cultures to create familiar
surroundings and to maintain, at least for a time, established patterns
of behaviour. Present indications, imprecise as they are, suggest that
with the passage of time these ethnic groups will become more dispersed in Melbourne's residential structure, as they have in other countries of immigration (Lieberson 1963:44-91). The rate of this dispersal
will, however, probably vary from one group to another, reflecting
differences in initial social and cultural distance from the receiving
society.

The extent of ethnic concentration in Melbourne can be assessed
from Fig. 5. As in previous sections, the factor coefficients for the first
component shown on Table 5.6 were used to calculate component scores
for each area. These scores, again in five quintile groups, are mapped on
Fig. 5. From this figure it is clear that the heaviest ethnic concentrations
are located in the inner city areas, north, south, and west of the city
centre—in Brunswick, Northcote, Carlton, Fitzroy, and Collingwood,
down through Richmond into South Melbourne and Port Melbourne,
and west from the city into Moonee Ponds, Essendon, and Footscray.
These were pre-eminently the areas of southern European concentration in Melbourne in 1961. The seven local government areas of the
City of Melbourne, Footscray, Essendon, Brunswick, Fitzroy, Collingwood, and Richmond alone contained almost 60,000 persons from
Italy, Greece, or Malta, a figure amounting to 17 per cent of the total
population of these same areas. The metropolitan average was only
6 per cent. In fact one in six of all the southern Europeans in Australia lived in one of these municipalities in 1961, compared with only
one in forty of the native-born population.

To illustrate the range of differences between areas in their ethnic
and religious composition, an abridged social profile is presented for
seven areas, selected on the same basis as in preceding chapters. The

five characteristics for which data are given represent the most important measures included in this component.

TABLE 5.7   Abridged ethnic profiles of seven residential areas, Melbourne, 1961

Area	% Catholic	% Orthodox	% born in Italy	% born in Australia	% alien nationals
517 (high ethnicity)	56	12	4	34	28
451	31	14	7	66	20
52	39	3	2	75	10
368	31	1	7	83	7
313	17	2	0	83	3
601	18	0	0	81	3
114 (low ethnicity)	12	0	0	92	1

The patterns depicted in Table 5.7 are not perhaps as systematic as those in previous chapters. The area with the highest ethnicity score is located not in the inner suburbs but on the western fringe of the metropolis, and interestingly enough it had relatively few Italian or Greek settlers. Although the figure for those of the Orthodox religion was very high, in fact only 2 per cent of the population were actually Greek-born. This suggests that the Orthodox figure in this case mainly comprises persons from eastern and central Europe. However, 13 per cent were Maltese-born, a figure very much higher than that for the city as a whole. But while the religious figures and the percentage Italian-born fluctuate somewhat as one progresses down the scale from high ethnicity to low ethnicity, the last two columns show much more systematic trends. An area in East Malvern had the lowest ethnicity score, and in this ACD only one in eight persons was a Catholic, a figure less than half the metropolitan average. Nine out of ten of its population were native-born, and of those born in other countries over half came from the United Kingdom. Only 2 per cent came from other European countries.

Although, as Fig. 5 makes clear, there were areas on the western fringe of the metropolis with high ethnicity, the most marked ethnic concentrations were located close to the city centre in areas with deteriorating housing and mixed land uses. To some extent the growth of ethnic concentrations has given these areas a new lease of life (Jones 1964), and even ten years ago Grant and Serle (1957:258) noted that many formerly dilapidated areas were breaking out in gay colours. Because of their concentration in the inner suburbs, areas with high ethnicity tend also to be areas of low familism. The correlation be-

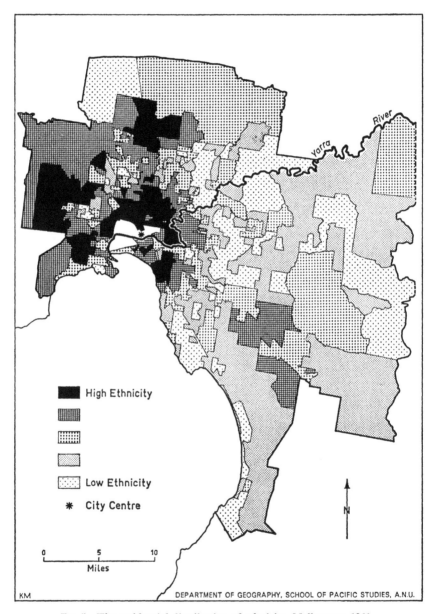

FIG. 5   The residential distribution of ethnicity, Melbourne, 1961

Key to Fig. 5

First quintile group (high ethnicity)

3	17	77	177	212	231	410	451	491	516
4	18	79	178	213	232	411	452	502	517
5	20	81	179	214	238	412	453	503	518
6	57	82	180	215	279	413	454	504	519
7	59	84	181	216	280	414	455	508	521
9	60	85	182	217	284	415	456	509	522
10	65	87	194	218	285	416	457	510	523
11	71	88	206	225	286	417	458	511	524
12	72	162	207	226	287	418	459	512	551
13	73	164	208	227	361	419	485	513	561
14	74	174	210	228	362	449	487	514	562
15	75	175	211	229	404	450	490	515	609
16	76								

Second quintile group

8	83	156	198	240	281	357	408	488	530
19	86	158	202	241	288	358	420	489	531
50	130	160	219	242	289	359	421	493	532
52	137	161	220	244	291	360	422	495	537
53	139	163	221	245	292	365	426	496	554
54	140	165	224	246	293	366	428	497	555
55	141	166	230	247	294	386	432	501	556
58	142	176	233	248	301	387	443	505	558
62	143	183	235	249	303	390	482	506	560
63	151	195	236	268	308	401	483	520	563
66	152	196	237	270	354	403	484	526	568
78	153	197	239	278	356	405	486	527	611
80	154								

Third quintile group

1	102	167	204	295	325	391	424	468	557
31	103	168	205	296	335	392	425	476	564
32	107	169	222	298	336	393	427	481	565
38	121	170	223	302	355	394	429	494	567
40	129	184	234	304	363	395	430	498	577
41	131	185	250	305	364	398	433	499	580
47	132	186	253	306	367	399	434	500	593
51	134	187	256	307	368	402	441	525	594
56	135	189	262	309	373	406	442	535	595
61	136	190	267	319	379	407	444	549	599
64	138	191	269	323	388	409	445	552	608
67	155	193	282	324	389	423	447	553	610
68	157	203							

Key to Fig. 5—*continued*

Fourth quintile group

2	89	125	199	297	329	369	400	492	579
25	94	126	200	300	330	371	431	529	585
27	95	127	243	312	333	372	436	533	589
28	98	128	252	313	334	375	437	534	590
30	100	133	254	314	337	378	440	538	591
33	101	145	255	315	338	381	446	543	597
34	104	148	257	317	342	382	448	544	598
37	108	159	258	318	347	383	461	550	600
39	109	172	260	322	348	384	462	566	604
42	111	173	261	326	350	385	463	573	605
43	120	188	283	327	352	396	466	575	606
44	122	192	290	328	353	397	471	576	607
46	123								

Fifth quintile group (low ethnicity)

21	90	115	201	275	340	380	474	542	581
22	91	116	209	276	341	435	475	545	582
23	92	117	251	277	343	438	477	546	583
24	93	118	259	299	344	439	478	547	584
26	96	119	263	310	345	460	479	548	586
29	97	124	264	311	346	464	480	559	587
35	99	144	265	316	349	465	507	569	588
36	105	146	266	320	351	467	528	570	592
45	106	147	271	321	370	469	536	571	596
48	110	149	272	331	374	470	539	572	601
49	112	150	273	332	376	472	540	574	602
69	113	171	274	339	377	473	541	578	603
70	114								

tween the familism scores of Chapter 4 and the ethnicity scores computed in this chapter is — 0·44. This finding cannot be taken as evidence of low fertility among ethnic groups, since indeed one of the highest loading measures in the ethnicity construct is percentage of Catholics, and we know that Catholics have higher fertility than non-Catholics (Day 1965). The relationship is rather an ecological one, reflecting a tendency for immigrants to settle disproportionately in the transitional zones of the city, where only a small proportion of the population consists of children under fifteen.

The relationship between ethnicity and socioeconomic status is rather stronger (r = — 0·64), and areas with high ethnicity tend also to be areas with low socioeconomic status. The interpretation of this relationship is more complex, and both ecological and individual characteristics need to be taken into account. Studies of social stratification in North America have shown conclusively that although economic class position and ethnic affiliation can be distinguished conceptually, in countries the economic and demographic growth of which has depended upon immigration the relationship between social class and ethnic origin is especially close. Porter (1965:73), for example, in his recent analysis of class and power in contemporary Canadian society, emphasised the interrelationship between ethnicity and social class, and found the hierarchical relationship between Canada's different cultural groups a recurring theme in his analysis.

> Immigration and ethnic affiliation (or membership in a cultural group) have been important factors in the formation of social classes in Canada. In particular, ethnic differences have been important in building up the bottom layer of the stratification system in both agricultural and industrial settings . . . Depending on the immigration period, some groups have assumed a definite 'entrance status'.

There can be no doubt that similar considerations apply in Australian society, but as yet a firm empirical base for making such statements is lacking. Nonetheless, it is clear that the immigration of certain groups is still viewed negatively by many Australians (Adler and Taft 1966:77) and that some ethnic groups have assumed a definite entrance status. The extent to which different ethnic groups occupy different positions in the social hierarchy is well illustrated by unpublished 1961 census data relating to birthplace and occupation. These data, currently being analysed in the Department of Sociology at the Australian National University, show that whereas only 9 per cent of Australian-born male workers described their occupation as 'labourer', among Greek-born workers the figure was as high as 31 per cent. The comparable figure for Italians was 28 per cent and for Poles 22 per cent.

Among the Dutch and Germans, however, the figure dropped to 10 and 11 per cent respectively, reflecting a higher proportion of craftsmen in these two groups. These figures are suggestive of the important interrelationship between social class, social prestige, and social power in Australia. The fact that such a relationship can be observed at the ecological level provides some measure of the extent to which these individual differences have been incorporated into the social differentiation of residential areas. It further reflects the concentration of non-British immigrants in areas of relatively low socioeconomic status. Obviously, time and social mobility will have an effect on this situation, but how much and how fast are questions to which we do not yet have answers. As more studies of residential concentration and occupational structure become available, some of these important questions will begin to be answered.

The comparison of these Melbourne findings with ethnic and religious groups elsewhere is obviously a necessary final task. It is unfortunately a very difficult one, as comparative studies of other Australian metropolises are not available. However, Zubrzycki's work on the 1954 census does show that even in the mid-1950s quite clear and in some cases marked areas of ethnic concentration existed in Sydney, Melbourne, Brisbane, and Adelaide (Zubrzycki 1960:79-85). Since 1954 the degree of ethnic concentration in Melbourne has been relatively stable, except among the Greeks, whose degree of concentration increased from slightly below to well above the level for Italians (see Table 5.4) (Jones 1967b). However, it should be emphasised that the measure of ethnic concentration used in this and many other studies does not take into account the absolute size of the group concerned but considers only its relative residential distribution compared with that of all the others. Obviously both the degree of concentration *and* the size of the group concerned are important factors in assessing the impact, or visibility, of an ethnic concentration. Even though the relative degree of residential concentration has not in recent years increased markedly among Melbourne's non-British settlers, the absolute size of such groups more than doubled between 1954 and 1961 to more than a quarter of a million. Even with no overall increase in concentration, the social impact of these concentrations was much more marked in Melbourne in 1961 than it was seven years before.

Compared with cities in the United States, the level of ethnic concentration in Melbourne seems rather similar. This generalisation must be subject to some qualifications. The most important qualification is that cultural and historical differences between Australia and the United States must influence the interpretation of any statistical comparison. In the United States the great wave of non-British immigration occurred in the first decade of this century, when attitudes towards immigrants were greatly different from those of today. Moreover, the immigrants themselves often came from countries the social structures of which have changed even more dramatically than those of the United States or Australia in the last half-century. In Australia, on the other hand, the mass migration of central, eastern, and southern Europeans has been primarily a post-World War II phenomenon. The social environment in which immigrants in the two countries have found themselves are rather different. In addition, there are statistical difficulties in the comparisons, because of difference in the size of residential areas used, in the ethnic composition of different cities, and so on. Accordingly the comparison I am about to offer can only be a very general one.

Recent evidence assembled by Lieberson (1963:45-8) indicates that in 1950 the average index of ethnic concentration for twelve foreign-born groups in ten American cities was 0·39, a figure which had declined somewhat from that of twenty years before (0·44 in 1930). The comparable 1961 figure for eight ethnic groups in Melbourne was 0·41. To match his comparison, I have included the British, New Zealand, German, Greek, Italian, Maltese, and Polish indexes of concentration, in this case indexes of dissimilarity. Since Lieberson's data were mainly derived from census tracts, which are on average slightly larger than the units used in this study, this small difference can be discounted. It seems fair to conclude that in terms simply of this statistical measure of ethnic concentration Melbourne does not appear to differ markedly from these American cities.

In the conclusion to Chapter 3 I pointed out that the degree of residential concentration among socioeconomic groups also seemed similar to that in American cities for which data are available. (I have been unable to find comparative data for familism.) However, there is one major difference between American and Australian metropolises, involving the residential concentration of racial groups. No statistics for Aborigines or Chinese were included in this study, so that I cannot say to what extent these groups are more or less segregated than the ethnic groups. Certainly, casual observation suggests a high degree of residential concentration, but then these are very small minorities, at least in the largest cities. There is no counterpart to the conspicuous and highly concentrated racial enclaves characteristic of many American cities.

Statistical information on Negro segregation in 207 American cities presented by the Taeubers provides striking evidence on this point

G

(Taeuber and Taeuber 1965:31-7). Half the cities considered had indexes of residential dissimilarity of over 0·88, figures which approach the theoretical maximum of this index. To achieve the same residential distribution as whites in these cities, nine out of ten Negroes would have had to move into different census tracts. An earlier study by Karl Taeuber of 1950 census data for 188 large cities showed that in 47 of these cities more than 25 per cent of the Negroes lived in city blocks that contained no white residents. In 186 of the 188 cities 50 per cent or more of the white population lived in all-white blocks. These figures are quoted not as an invidious comparison, but simply to indicate an important dimension of social and residential differentiation largely, but not entirely, absent from Australian cities. Lest the point be mistaken as patriotic self-congratulation, perhaps I can conclude this section by drawing attention to the close similarity between the degree of residential segregation in the two countries in those two dimensions where comparisons are possible—socioeconomic status and ethnicity. In view of this similarity, it is sobering, if as yet speculative, to think about what might occur in Australian cities if substantial numbers of non-Europeans resided in them. Is the difference only one of magnitude, in the relative size of the non-European population in Australia and the United States? Perhaps as Australia's indigenous minority, the Aborigines, grow in number and become increasingly urbanised we will have an answer to this critical question.

6

A Classification of Residential Areas

Before proceeding to develop a classification or typology of Melbourne's residential areas, it may be useful to summarise what has emerged out of the preceding analysis. The discussion presented so far has been designed to demonstrate three main things. The first and most fundamental aim has been to demonstrate in as concise terms as possible that considerable diversity exists among the different residential areas of Melbourne. People living in some parts of the city have quite different social characteristics from those in other parts. Although in this study our attention has been focused on one particular city, it is clear that similar differences could be, and are being, documented in other Australian metropolises. No matter what characteristic is selected for analysis, quite striking differences can usually be identified. There are areas, for example, where detached private houses predominate and areas where almost everyone lives in flats; areas where a substantial section of the population derives from overseas countries of origin and areas where almost everyone was born in Australia, Britain, or New Zealand; areas where there are few children and others where half the population consists of children still at school; areas with largely Protestant populations and areas where Catholics predominate. And so we could go on.

The documentation of this striking diversity was an initial task. A second and equally important question is how we can best describe and analyse the variation that exists between the populations of all the residential areas in a city. One can consider individual characteristics in isolation, as discrete pieces of information interesting in themselves, and simply identify areas where young children, old people, the rich, the poor, the native-born, the foreign-born, or any other groups are particularly heavily concentrated. Such an approach provides information that is not only interesting in itself but also of practical importance in planning the distribution of social services or other community facilities. Such a goal is not at all incompatible with the methods adopted in this study. A substantial amount of such useful information was provided in the course of this report. Town planners themselves frequently conduct such analyses, not always with the conservative aim of accommodating future patterns of growth and future community demands. Very often the study of what exists now and is likely to exist in the future necessitates more radical planning designed to alter existing patterns and the course of future development. My point is that, whatever the precise goal of urban planning, it must begin from an understanding of the existing situation and of the factors that give rise to it.

An alternative, or perhaps supplementary, approach, which has guided most of this analysis, is to view these various social and residential differences not as discrete items of information but in terms of more general factors or organising constructs. In the present study I have tried to show that one useful means of organising the extensive array of information on urban social and residential differentiation is to order it by means of three constructs—socioeconomic status, household composition, and ethnicity—constructs derived with modifications from the researches of Eshref Shevky and his associates. The preceding chapters have attempted to evaluate the usefulness of this scheme of analysis, and in successive sections many social and demographic characteristics relating to small residential areas in Melbourne have been analysed. Components, or factors, were identified which corresponded closely to those suggested by the research and theoretical formulations of social area analysts. I did, however, emphasise that this result was partly determined by the mode of analysis. Because the analysis was structured according to certain expectations, it was in a sense inevitable that the three general factors which I was seeking would emerge. Indeed, it would have been surprising if a component analysis of twenty-four socioeconomic measures had not given rise to a socioeconomic component.

While this qualification needs to be stated, it does not in my view detract at all from the usefulness of this approach. What is most important for our purposes is not that components equivalent to Shevky's social rank, urbanisation, and segregation could be identified in successive analyses, but that in each case these components were by far the most dominant ones. This result assumes even greater importance when it is remembered that the second component in the socioeconomic status domain was apparently a measure of urbanisation and that the second component in the urbanisation domain was an indirect measure of socioeconomic status. This overlapping, or lack of unidimensionality, is only to be expected in a pioneering exploration of the interrelationships of many variables. The results of this study should mean that future studies will be able to rely upon a much narrower range of measures. To some extent it will be necessary to incorporate additional and possibly even more effective measures of social differentiation. From the 1966 census it will be possible to obtain CD data on occupation, education, household and family composition, and the type of materials used in the construction of dwellings. Residents of Melbourne will know that the socioeconomic status level of areas is reflected in building materials. In some suburbs cheaper timber and fibro houses predominate, while in other areas most houses are of brick construction. Unfortunately, in the 1961 census information on the materials of outer walls of dwellings was not available for CDs. It is available, however, for local government areas.

Although I have argued that the results of the present study support the general suppositions underlying social area analysis, with the qualifications indicated in earlier chapters, it should be stressed that other types of social and residential differentiation were also identified which were not effectively accounted for by the three general dimensions of socioeconomic status, household composition, and ethnicity. In the analysis of ethnic and religious differences three—not one—distinct patterns of ethnic differentiation emerged. Likewise, several measures in the socioeconomic and demographic clusters showed independent patterns of variation. But while this finding is important, it is not at all incompatible with our general orientation, which simply states that these three dimensions of differentiation are the most salient axes along which urban populations in modern industrial societies become socially and residentially differentiated. They are not the only ones. Indeed, in some cities at given points of time additional unique factors may also be important. Moreover, in ethnically homogeneous societies the ethnic dimension will obviously be unimportant, and other types of subcultural variation—for example urban-rural migrants—may need to be taken into account. But by employing the method of component analysis on separate clusters of characteristics, it becomes possible to identify not only these basic dimensions of differentiation, but the less important ones as well.

Once the internal diversity of urban populations has been documented, and once reliable and succinct means of summarising and interpreting that diversity have been developed, there remains a third task, that of classification. What patterns of social differentiation occur with the greatest frequency? What relationships characterise different areas of the city, and do these relationships change significantly as we move from one district of the city to another? How systematic are the residential differences that can be distinguished, and what do these systematic patterns suggest about the social structure of the city itself? These are some of the questions that this chapter sets out to answer.

From a statistical point of view any system of classification involves three terms: the objects that are to be classified (in this instance the residential areas of a city), the information about them which might serve as the basis of such a classification, and the uses to which the classification is to be put. Let us briefly consider the last two terms first.

The information that is available about the residential areas of any modern industrial city is so vast as to be in principle infinite. It would be possible to go on indefinitely amassing 'relevant' data about them, a prospect that may one day be a reality if urban data banks come into existence. It goes without saying that data banks in themselves will not provide solutions to any social problems. They will simply remove one obstacle to their solution—lack of information. In practice the information available to any researcher is limited, since no use can be made of information we do not as yet possess. In the present study attention was limited to 1961 census data. This choice does not imply that other information is irrelevant to the study of urban social and residential structure, or even that urban social structure can be exhaustively analysed by means of census data relating to the resident populations of small geographic units in the city. However, we do claim that the residential area represents a social environment which reflects and in turn influences the behaviour of urbanites. By analysing the ways in which these social environments differ we can learn a great deal about urban social processes. An understanding of such processes leads not only to useful knowledge about residential areas as such but also to expectations about individual behaviour that can then be investigated by other techniques.

The classification developed in these chapters does not utilise all the census data analysed in preceding sections, but is based on the three derived constructs of socioeconomic status, household composition, and ethnicity. Let us say at once that since these three constructs have been shown to summarise effectively a considerable range of information about residential areas, such a classification will have numerous applications. It can be used as a framework within which other studies of urban behaviour can be conducted, as a means of identifying recurrent modes of social differentiation and social organisation, and as a source for specific hypotheses about the social structure of Australian cities. Because this study is the first major study of its kind published for any Australian metropolis, its full utility will be more adequately appreciated when the results of companion studies become available. A comparative study of the residential structure of Australian metropolises, and a comparison of Melbourne in 1966 or 1971 with the Melbourne of 1961, will undoubtedly give a sharper edge to the findings of the present study.

Put briefly, then, the present classification has been developed for many purposes rather than in relation to one specific objective. It is based on three general dimensions of social and residential differentiation which jointly explain a large amount of the variation among many social and demographic characteristics. Although as a general classification it is basically descriptive, it will also have considerable predictive value. The groupings provided by it will prove to be associated with other behavioural characteristics not used in deriving the classification itself. In concrete terms, information on the relative levels of socioeconomic status, familism, and ethnicity in different areas of the city will have predictive value for the study of such matters as poverty, mental illness, social and ethnic stratification, patterns of expenditure and consumption, crime and social deviance generally, family and household differentials, voting behaviour and political attitudes, membership of social and community groups, and a whole range of social-psychological phenomena. The practical applications of such research in town planning and social administration are obvious, and indeed much of the impetus for such studies overseas has arisen out of the information requirements of town planners and social administrators responsible for the provision of urban services.

One difficulty in applying the results of the present study is that the areas I have used (aggregations of CDs) do not as they stand conform to more generally used geographical frames of reference, such as suburbs or postal districts. They do, of course, add to form local government areas, and in Appendix II have listed all 611 ACDs sequentially by local government area. I have also included a key which identifies the ACDs contained in a list of 136 Melbourne postal districts for which precise boundaries could be obtained. This information, together with the base map (Fig. 10), should be sufficient to identify most areas quite accurately.

Before describing this classification of ACDs a small diversion is required. In the conclusion to the preceding chapter, it was mentioned that moderate associations existed between the three dimensions of socioeconomic status, household composition, and ethnicity. Is it therefore really necessary to use three dimensions, or can an even smaller number of concepts be employed to account for most social differences between residential areas in Melbourne equally well? One possible way of answering this question is to restructure the previous analysis by taking a number of measures from each of the three dimensions and subjecting them to an overall component analysis. This in effect changes our model of analysis from one where we specify in advance the main clusters of variables to a model where these clusters will be allowed to emerge empirically. Instead of simply considering correlations between measures within each separate domain, correlations between domains can be considered as well. This analytic model is in fact that most commonly used in factor analytic studies, where no *a priori* grouping of measures into clusters is generally attempted before embarking upon the factor analysis itself.

There is no difficulty in adopting such a strategy. In fact a correlation matrix was calculated for a new set of twenty-four measures, new not because they were not analysed before but because eight are derived from each of the three dimensions of socioeconomic status, familism, and ethnicity. In general measures correlating highly with the first component in each dimension were selected, but where lower order components had a clear meaning one or two measures associated with those components were also included—for example the masculinity rate and the percentages in the Lutheran, Jewish, and Dutch categories. The rates of population change and population density were also included because they are frequently used in studies of urban form and structure. Table 6.1 lists the twenty-four measures selected, together with the factor coefficients for the first three components. The correlation matrix from which this table was calculated has not been reproduced, as this section of the analysis is mainly illustrative.

The results of Table 6.1 are clear enough. Socioeconomic status and ethnicity collapse into a single component, accounting for just over one-third of the total variance. As the pattern of factor coefficients shows, the heaviest loadings for the first component come from the first and third clusters, where all except four measures have coefficients of 0·7 or greater. In the socioeconomic cluster, only the percentage of owner-occupied houses has a loading below this figure, and the remaining three measures are all from the ethnicity cluster. None of these three (Lutheran, Jewish, and Dutch) was originally associated with the factor termed 'general ethnic composition'; all emerged rather as distinct patterns of ethnic concentration (Table 5.6). The fact that the analytically distinct dimensions of socioeconomic status and ethnicity coalesce empirically into a single component illustrates very strikingly the existence of ethnic stratification in Australia and the extent to which ethnic and religious differences have been incorporated into the social stratification and residential differentiation of urban populations. The pattern of coefficients associated with the first component of Table 6.1 also reinforces the earlier finding that areas with high socioeconomic status tend to be areas of low ethnicity.

TABLE 6.1 Factor coefficients between 24 socioeconomic, demographic, and ethnic characteristics and three principal components

| Characteristic | Factor coefficients for components | | |
	SES[a] ethnicity	Familism	Northwestern European settlers
Socioeconomic status			
1 % MWF employers	0·71	−0·47	0·18
2 % MWF not at work	−0·82	−0·14	0·01
3 % MWF in finance and property	0·84	−0·34	0·02
4 % MWF in commerce	0·71	−0·42	−0·15
5 % MWF in business and community services	0·74	−0·39	0·14
6 % FWF in manufacturing	−0·75	0·50	−0·06
7 % owner-occupied houses	0·53	0·29	0·36
8 Education ratio	0·71	−0·43	0·22
Familism			
9 % population 0-14	0·17	0·93	−0·11
10 % never-married adults	−0·28	−0·88	−0·05
11 % population male	−0·30	0·26	−0·25
12 % widowed	−0·08	−0·90	−0·06
13 % females in workforce	−0·57	−0·74	0·08
14 % private houses	0·30	0·77	−0·20
15 % population change	0·06	0·69	0·20
16 Population density	−0·54	−0·51	−0·28
Ethnicity			
17 % Catholic	−0·87	0·04	0·04
18 % Orthodox	−0·74	−0·23	0·24
19 % Lutheran	−0·09	0·09	0·81
20 % Presbyterian	0·86	−0·03	0·08
21 % Hebrew	0·19	−0·70	0·04
22 % Italian-born	−0·76	−0·15	0·25
23 % Netherlands-born	0·20	0·31	0·63
24 % alien nationals	−0·78	−0·15	0·50
Eigenvalue (V_p)	8·50	6·32	1·93
100 $V_p/24$	35·42	26·33	8·04

[a]SES = socioeconomic status.

Although according to Table 6.1 socioeconomic status and ethnicity collapse empirically into one component, household composition (familism) emerges as an independent component accounting for about 25 per cent of the original variance. Its factor loadings are much as we would expect, with one interesting extension. The Jews, whose residential pattern gave rise to a separate component in the ethnic analysis, are now included in the familism dimension. This suggests, not that Jews themselves have low familism, but that they live in areas characterised by low familism, the areas of high urbanisation a few miles south and east of the city centre. This was indeed the case. To take only one example, in ACD 503 in St Kilda 28 per cent of the population belonged to the Jewish religion. This area contained few private houses, few children, but many young unmarried adults. As Appendix I shows, it had the thirty-seventh lowest familism score in the city.

The third component of Table 6.1 largely repeats the third component of the preceding chapter, and identifies areas with high proportions of settlers from northwestern Europe. Scores computed on this component correlated + 0·75 with those calculated from the third component of Table 5.6. The familism scores correlated + 0·91 with those derived in Chapter 4, and the socioeconomic status/ethnicity scores correlated 0·88 and − 0·76 respectively with the socioeconomic status and ethnicity scores derived above. Clearly the fit between these measures is very close, despite differences in the choice of primary data.

It would have been possible to derive a classification of Melbourne's residential areas from only the first two components of Table 6.1. Indeed, that was my original intention, partly because it involved fewer operations and provided a means of weighting the different components (Jones 1968). However, there is one critical argument against such a procedure. Component analysis, like factor analysis, is only an analytic tool. It is a very powerful method of analysis but is not a substitute for theory. It is possible, even popular to judge from the expanding literature based on such methods of analysis (Hadden and Borgatta 1965; Schmid and Tagashira 1964; Sweetser 1965; Jones 1965), to correlate a large number of more or less arbitrarily selected measures, apply factor analytic methods to the correlation matrix, and extract complex factor patterns either in a purely empirical way or by the routine application of specific factor models.

There is unfortunately no sound reason to expect meaningful results to emerge from such analyses. Often some of the factors retained for rotation will have little explanatory power, and the factor solutions obtained are not unique. Changes in the number of factors retained for rotation can have marked effects on the results (Cartwright 1965). Moreover, the choice of one rather than another factor model needs to be justified, and it remains to be shown that the notion of 'simple structure' even applies in fields other than that for which it was originally hypothesised—the study of the factors of the mind. It seems to me that the application of powerful analytic techniques means that more attention rather than less has to be given to the role of theory in arriving at meaningful formulations of research objectives. The application of increasingly sophisticated techniques of analysis provides in itself no guarantee that the results they produce will be meaningful.

Viewed in this light the type of analysis reported in Table 6.1 owes little to systematic theory. It takes twenty-four measures, applies a mathematical technique of analysis, and extracts a number of summarising components in terms of which the original measures can be more simply understood. At precisely this point of interpretation an important problem arises. Conceptually distinct types of social and residential differentiation may be empirically so closely intertwined that this method of analysis cannot separate them.* The question then becomes one of theoretical judgment, whether the empirical relationship overrides the conceptual distinction (is it a useful distinction?), or whether the observed relationship simply adds to our understanding of how these concepts 'work' in a specific social system. Granted that in an overall component analysis of these Melbourne data the strength of the empirical link between socioeconomic status and ethnicity produces a generalised component spanning both these dimensions, the question is—do we want such a joint measure or should we seek separate measures of each dimension? (Jones 1967d).

The preference in this study, as the reader will probably have inferred, is for separate measures of conceptually distinct dimensions. This preference was not clearly perceived from the outset but emerged gradually, partly from the attempt to make sense of the data and partly from discussions of preliminary findings. Initially a classification using only two scores was derived. However, the advantage of being able to compare residential areas along all three dimensions of differentiation, whatever the empirical relationships between them, was judged the most important consideration. As we shall see, there are some areas in Melbourne which depart significantly from what might be expected on the basis of a more general analysis. Moreover, by retaining separate measures of each concept we can assess long-term trends in the relationships among them, and compare the situation in Melbourne with other Australian metropolises.

How then was a classification of Melbourne's social areas derived? The method can probably be best explained by an analogy. Imagine a large, hollow glass cube with transparent sides. The width of the cube can be visualised as representing socioeconomic status, the depth household composition, and the height ethnicity. Inside this cube are

---

* If I appear to ignore so-called oblique factor solutions it is by design, not ignorance. I am doubtful whether they offer a better solution to this problem than my strategy of structuring the initial analysis according to *a priori* expectations.

suspended numerous glass beads, each representing a single residential area. Let us imagine further that all the 611 'beads' of this study have been suspended inside this glass cube. Some of them will be close together, clumped in tight clusters of different size, others will be spread out between groups. Areas with high socioeconomic status will cluster on the left-hand side of the cube, those with low familism will be towards the back, and areas with high ethnicity will be closer to the top than the bottom.

Even though some parts of the interior of this cube will be quite densely packed, the pattern of distribution will obviously be very complex. How are we to identify groups of areas with 'similar' patterns of scores? Fortunately, the development of high-speed computers and advances in numerical techniques of classification have made several solutions to this problem practicable. The method adopted in this study involves the calculation of a distance coefficient—the coefficient of Squared Euclidean Distance (Moser and Scott 1961:80-2). By this technique all possible pairs of areas are compared. The two most similar areas are identified and are replaced by one new area with scores halfway between the original ones—the so-called centroid method (Williams and Lance 1965). To give an example from this study, distance coefficients for all possible pairs of areas were calculated (there were initially 186,355 such coefficients). The two areas with the smallest coefficient were then fused to form a new area, with new scores representing the arithmetic mean of the original scores. After each fusion, the number of areas remaining to be grouped, or classified, decrease by one (since two old areas have become one new area). Thus, if there are N objects to be grouped, then N−1 fusions of this type will be required to group them. The result is a hierarchical set of groupings, or family tree, such as that shown in Fig. 6.

The first two areas to be combined by this method were ACDs 356 (in Northcote) and 555 (in Williamstown), for which scores on the socioeconomic status, familism, and ethnicity components were −101 and −101, −93 and −91, and 79 and 82 respectively—that is, comparatively low scores on the first two scales and somewhat higher than average on the third. The mean of all scales is zero, and high positive scores indicate high positions on all scales (see Appendix I). For those interested in the mathematics of it, the coefficient of Squared Euclidean Distance (SED) is calculated as follows:

$$\text{SED} = (x_i - x_j)^2 + (y_i - y_j)^2 + (z_i - z_j)^2$$

where x_i and x_j are scores on the first component, y_i and y_j those for the second component, and z_i and z_j those for the third component, for areas i and j respectively. For the two areas mentioned above, the calculations were:

$$SED = [(-101) - (-101)]^2 + [(-93) - (-91)]^2 + [79 - 82]^2$$
$$= 0 + 4 + 9$$
$$= 13$$

Thus, ACDs 356 and 555 disappear from the analysis and in their place stands a new 'area' 612, with scores of — 101, —92, and 80·5. This process continues, and gradually new groups are built up *seriatim*. The last ACD to be grouped was an area in Fitzroy (ACD 218), which had low socioeconomic status, very low familism, and very high ethnicity.

Fig. 6 shows the hierarchy of groups which emerged out of this analysis. The composition of these groups is given in keys to Figs. 7, 8, and 9, and Table 6.2 provides some summary characteristics by means of which the salient characteristics of each group can be assessed. One difficulty, even with this type of classification, is deciding how many groups should be distinguished. Fig. 6 shows the final fusions of the twenty highest order groupings. That is to say, at this level of the analysis the original 611 areas had already been combined into twenty groups—some large, some small, some consisting even of one ACD if it was sufficiently dissimilar from other areas in the city.

Several comments about Fig. 6 are required. Why twenty groups? Why not twenty-five, or fifteen, or some other number? The number twenty was selected arbitrarily as an initial compromise between too many and too few groups. Since the major aim of this typology was to provide a concise and economical description of initially complex patterns, more than twenty groups would have been cumbersome. It is in any case always possible to identify the outlying members of a group by examining the scores of its constituent members. If twenty groups is considered too many, a smaller number of groups can be easily selected at a higher level in the hierarchy. In the present analysis these twenty groups can be reduced to eight (1208, 1212, 1214, 1211, 1207, 1209, 1210, 1213), or, at an even higher level of generality, to three (1215, 1217, 1218). It is possible to select any set of groupings with differing degrees of internal similarity. Obviously the more general the grouping the greater is the degree of internal variability.

Fig. 6 gives no indication of the size of each group or its social composition. Table 6.2 gives some of this information. The groups are shown in the same order as on the diagram, and to aid interpretation I have shown for each group its mean rank position on each scale and also its type. This type was derived in the following way. All the areas

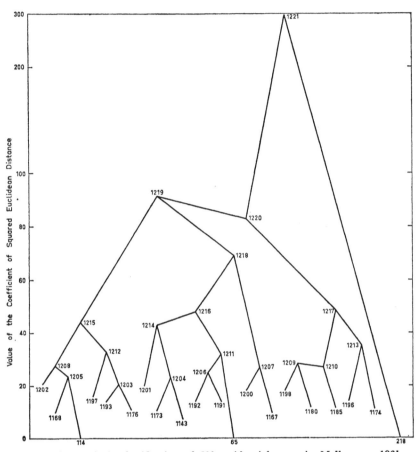

Fɪɢ. 6   An intrinsic classification of 611 residential areas in Melbourne, 1961

in the city were ranked according to their scores on a particular scale and divided into four equal groups (quartiles). The first group was designated double plus, the second plus, the third minus, and the fourth double minus. Since a high score means high socioeconomic status, high familism, or high ethnicity, as the case may be, this type designation locates the characteristics of each group by its relation to the average for all areas in the city.

At this stage it will be helpful if we can identify the relative location of these areas in Melbourne. Figs. 7, 8, and 9 map all twenty groups. Because the detail is rather too great for a single diagram, three balancing maps have been prepared, one for each of the three high order groupings (1215, 1218, and 1217). In the discussion that follows we will need to take into account these three figures and Table 6.2, and

TABLE 6.2 Summary profiles of 20 groups of residential areas

Group	SES		Familism		Ethnicity		Number of areas
	Mean rank score	Type[a]	Mean rank score	Type	Mean rank score	Type	
1202	375	+	450	+	158	−	183
1168	567	+ +	534	+ +	61	− −	14
114	598	+ +	435	+	1	− −	1
1197	519	+ +	225	−	176	−	81
1193	244	−	209	−	119	− −	4
1176	301	−	330	+	15	− −	3
1201	37	− −	602	+ +	320	+	8
1173	152	− −	494	+ +	407	+	41
1143	226	−	601	+ +	342	+	3
1192	30	− −	463	+ +	545	+ +	14
1191	8	− −	483	+ +	607	+ +	5
65	36	− −	606	+ +	563	+ +	1
1200	128	− −	518	+ +	18	− −	6
1167	37	− −	437	+	149	− −	5
1198	493	+ +	7	− −	370	+	7
1180	477	+ +	77	− −	402	+	47
1185	265	−	32	− −	503	+ +	27
1196	101	− −	144	− −	537	+ +	94
1174	215	−	254	−	362	+	66
218	57	− −	2	− −	606	+ +	1

[a] Symbols in 'type' columns are as follows:
+ + = first quartile group (very high)
+ = second quartile group (higher than average)
− = third quartile group (lower than average)
− − = fourth quartile group (very low)

for those who are concerned with even more detail, Appendix I as well.

Let us take each major group in turn. Table 6.2 shows that the groups differ markedly in size. Some consist of only one original area, while others contain over one hundred ACDs. To some extent this variation in size is an artefact of our cutting point. Group 1202, for example, would have been rather smaller if we had looked at the last twenty-five groups or so. In fact, in the key to Fig. 7 I have divided this group into two, and thirty-four areas with rather higher socio-economic status and lower ethnicity than the other areas in Group 1202 have been distinguished (Group 1202A).

Almost one-third of the areas included in this study are placed in Group 1202. In general they are characterised by slightly higher than

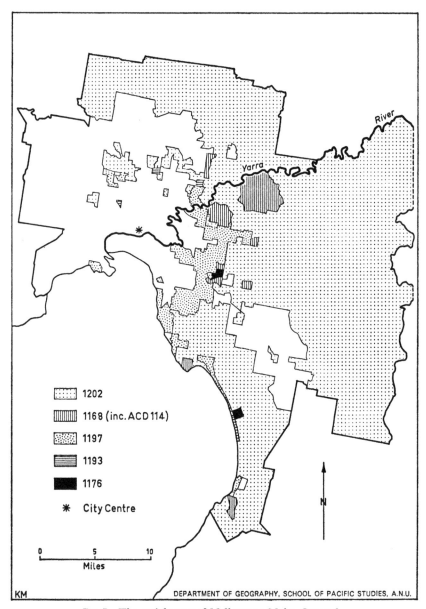

FIG. 7   The social areas of Melbourne: Major Group 1

Key to Fig. 7

Group 1202A[a]

21	29	98	192	264	326	344	376	473	573
23	48	99	201	266	332	346	465	569	587
24	49	119	252	311	343	349	472	572	603
26	70	123	257						

Group 1202B

22	156	261	328	354	384	444	533	575	592
25	168	272	333	368	385	446	536	576	593
27	169	274	334	369	388	447	538	577	594
28	171	275	335	370	389	448	539	579	595
30	172	283	336	371	392	460	543	580	596
31	173	317	337	372	396	461	544	581	597
34	187	318	338	373	397	462	545	582	598
51	188	319	339	375	398	463	546	583	601
56	253	320	340	377	400	464	547	584	604
68	254	321	341	378	423	466	549	585	605
69	255	322	342	379	431	467	550	586	606
145	256	323	345	380	436	477	566	588	607
146	258	324	351	381	438	480	570	589	608
149	259	325	352	382	439	492	571	590	610
150	260	327	353	383	440	500	574	591	

Group 1168

89	91	96	114[b]	312	474	475	548	578	602
90	95	97	251						

Group 1197

32	45	102	112	125	193	290	306	330	470
33	46	104	113	126	199	296	307	331	471
35	47	105	115	127	200	297	310	347	476
36	92	106	116	128	203	298	313	348	478
37	93	108	120	129	243	299	314	350	479
39	94	109	121	131	262	300	315	406	507
42	100	110	122	133	263	302	316	407	559
43	101	111	124	144	265	305	329	469	600
44									

Group 1193

148	159	209	277

Group 1176

117	118	147

[a] The areas in this group have higher average socioeconomic status and lower average ethnicity than areas in Group 1202B.

[b] Group 114 (one area) is included with Group 1168 (14 areas).

H

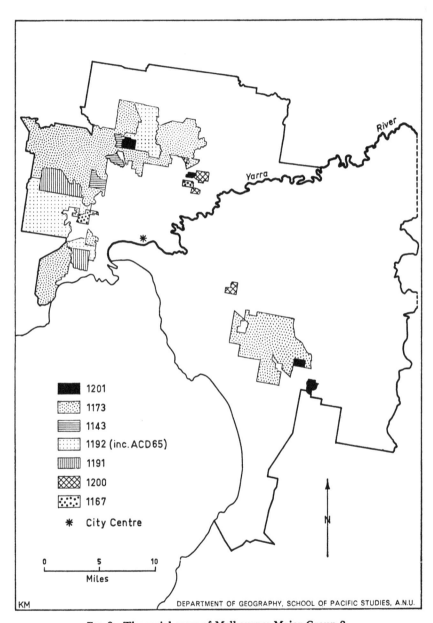

Fig. 8   The social areas of Melbourne: Major Group 2

Key to Fig. 8

Group 1201

| 61 | 62 | 63 | 64 | 191 | 437 | 567 | 568 | | |

Group 1173

52	66	184	278	284	391	433	493	497	537
53	165	190	279	386	393	434	494	498	563
54	166	235	280	387	401	443	495	499	609
55	167	238	281	390	432	445	496	526	611
58									

Group 1143

| 50 | 67 | 282 |

Group 1192

| 57 | 60 | 219 | 519 | 521 | 523 | 524 | 527 | 551 | 561 |
| 59 | 65ᵃ | 518 | 520 | 522 | | | | | |

Group 1191

| 285 | 286 | 287 | 517 | 562 |

Group 1200

| 271 | 273 | 276 | 540 | 541 | 542 |

Group 1167

| 424 | 435 | 528 | 529 | 534 |

ᵃ Group 65 (one area) included with Group 1192 (14 areas).

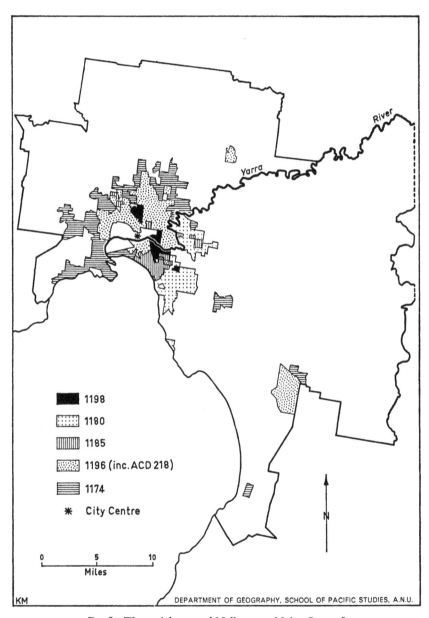

FIG. 9   The social areas of Melbourne: Major Group 3

Key to Fig. 9

Group 1198

1	2	14	19	409	421	481

Group 1180

38	130	137	142	246	291	301	408	501	506
40	132	138	143	248	292	303	420	503	509
41	134	139	239	249	293	304	422	504	510
103	135	140	242	250	294	308	468	505	514
107	136	141	245	268	295	309			

Group 1185

18	240	247	412	417	482	487	508	512	515
196	241	410	414	418	483	488	511	513	516
207	244	411	416	419	484	502			

Group 1196

3	13	76	151	178	208	218[a]	232	413	456
4	15	77	152	179	210	220	358	415	457
5	16	79	160	180	211	221	360	449	458
6	17	81	161	181	212	225	361	450	459
7	20	82	162	182	213	226	362	451	485
8	71	83	164	183	214	227	365	452	486
9	72	84	174	194	215	228	366	453	489
10	73	85	175	197	216	229	403	454	490
11	74	87	176	198	217	231	404	455	491
12	75	88	177	206					

Group 1174

78	158	202	233	270	364	425	441	535	557
80	163	204	234	289	367	426	442	552	558
86	170	205	236	355	394	427	525	553	560
153	185	222	237	356	395	428	530	554	564
154	186	223	267	357	399	429	531	555	565
155	189	224	268	359	402	430	532	556	599
157	195	230	269	363	405				

[a] Group 218 (one area) included with Group 1196 (94 areas).

average socioeconomic status and familism, and by low ethnicity. Although this group may be artificially large because of the ways the groups were chosen, in an important sense the size of this group reflects the fact that it comprises the areas of residence of the large and increasing urban middle classes. These are the areas where the families of native-born Australians enjoying average to better than average economic circumstances live, each in a modest but comfortable detached cottage not very different from the one next door. The size and importance of this segment of the urban population is well reflected in the attention it attracts from the advertising men, and in their stereotypical portrayal of their needs, hopes, and desires in a hundred television commercials commending the latest detergent, newest consumer appliance, and a myriad of other household objects. Their lives centre on family, leisure, home, and work, probably in that order. They live comfortably in middle class suburbs settled largely since the war, or perhaps in an older, more established area into which younger families are moving once again. During the week the man of the house works his thirty-five or forty hours, with perhaps a little overtime to buy an extra luxury. He probably is a small businessman, clerk, or skilled tradesman, and thinks of himself as middle class, or upper working class, depending on his family background. His wife, for he is typically married, probably spends her week raising his children, and when they reach school age spends her new-found leisure in more social activities—perhaps a sporting club or charitable work. She is more likely to see herself as middle class. At night they watch television for a few hours—probably a commercial channel—and weekends are occupied in the garden, on the golf course, perhaps by a drive in the family car to the pleasant hill country nearby in winter or the beach in summer. This is admittedly a speculative and perhaps too sharply drawn picture. But it seems fair to suggest that this group typifies the life style of suburban Australia, a way of life to which the mass of Australians aspire.

As an example of such an area we can take ACD 381 in an eastern suburb twelve or thirteen miles from the city centre. By 1961 it was relatively established, and its population had grown only slightly since 1954. Like most of these outer suburbs, almost all (95 per cent) of the houses were private houses set on quarter-acre lots at the low population density of 3,500 persons to the square mile. More than nine out of ten of these houses were owned or being purchased by their occupants. One in three persons was a child under the age of fifteen, and comparatively few—about one adult woman in six—was at work. Most of them were probably teenagers or young married women without any children. About one-third of the men worked in manufacturing industry, and one in nine of the male workforce was an employer or self-employed. One-quarter of those children between the ages of fifteen and twenty were still receiving full-time education. In all these respects this area conformed rather closely to the metropolitan norm. In religious and ethnic characteristics, however, it differed markedly from the metropolitan norm. Only 17 per cent were Catholics. Eighty-two per cent were born in Australia, and half the remainder came from the United Kingdom. Fewer than one in sixty persons had been born in southern Europe, compared with one in sixteen in the city as a whole.

Figures such as these are reasonably typical of most of the areas in Group 1202. Some have higher socioeconomic status, some lower. Others have more children and younger age structures, and some vary in their ethnic and religious composition. How much variation exists can be seen from the detailed figures given in Appendix I. Some areas with scores that differ markedly from the group averages are obviously outlying members of this group. I have tried to indicate only the central characteristics of this quite large group. Fig. 7 shows that the bulk of these areas lie east of the city centre. They begin about eight to nine miles out and extend to the edge of the metropolis.* Comparatively few areas in this group are north or west of the River Yarra (fewer than one in four), and most of those that are form a narrow, more or less continuous belt from Ivanhoe, through Preston and Reservoir, across to Pascoe Vale South, Essendon, and North Essendon. The latter areas tend to be older-established middle class areas undergoing transition. Those in Ivanhoe are in a newer, rapidly developing district along the heights bordering the northern bank of the Yarra.

As the classificatory diagram shows, the group with the most similar profile to Group 1202 is 1168. This group consists of only fourteen areas, but we can also conveniently consider ACD 114 with this group. (It has somewhat lower familism and ethnicity scores, but fuses with Group 1168 at the next highest level in the hierarchy.) These fifteen areas are unusual in that they combine a high level of socioeconomic status with high familism. They are in fact areas occupied by the affluent young, by the rising executives and professionals whose talents earn them high rewards in our technocratic society. While in age and family type they differ little from many of the areas in Group 1202, they live in larger houses—perhaps architect-designed—and have bigger

---

* Many of the fringe areas have low population densities, so that the visual impression given by this map may be a little misleading. The pattern of residential density can be inferred from the base map (Fig. 10).

and less 'popular' makes of car. They smoke more expensive cigarettes, and if we are to believe the stereotypes of the mass media they even have prettier wives and more tractable children. So much for the images. Obviously people with such characteristics live in many different parts of the city. Yet in some areas they are sufficiently numerous to constitute a modal type. As an example we can take ACD 90, an area which doubled its population between 1954 and 1961. Practically all the dwellings were owner-occupied private houses (95 per cent). Eight out of ten persons were under forty-five, and for every worker there were two dependants. One in five of the men at work were either employers or self-employed, and one in two worked in finance and property, commerce, public authority, or business and community services. There were more Presbyterians than Catholics, and 89 per cent were born in Australia. Half the foreign-born came from England, and only one in fifty was a national of a non-British country. If asked their social class, the residents of such an area would probably say 'middle', but a closer probing might elicit 'upper middle'.

The next group, 1197, is a much larger one containing eighty-one areas. As Table 6.2 suggests, this group is broadly similar in terms of socioeconomic status and ethnicity to many of the areas in the groups discussed above, but they have lower familism. Fig. 7 makes these differences a little clearer by showing that most of these areas are somewhat closer to the city centre or to major transportation routes. Being older-established areas, their populations are also a little older. They form a continuous block beginning just north of the Yarra extending south in a broad band through middle distance suburbs down to Port Phillip Bay. A few areas in this group are northwest or further south of the city centre. By and large these areas represent the established middle and upper middle class districts—established areas with established families, not so far out as those in the other groups and consequently likely to contain a slightly, but only slightly, higher proportion of immigrants. If we had to select an area representative of this group, we might take ACD 133. The population of this area changed little between the two censuses, at least in terms of its total size, and although most of the dwellings were private houses, one in eight was a shared house or a flat. Only 19 per cent of the population were children under fifteen, a number almost balanced by the percentage who were sixty-five or older (16 per cent). Eighty-four per cent were born in Australia, which, while slightly lower than in some areas of groups 1202 and 1168, is still well above the metropolitan average of 77 per cent. Sixteen per cent of male workers were employers or self-employed, a figure which is indicative of the high socioeconomic status of residents in this and other areas in this group. The areas with the highest socioeconomic status level in Melbourne—ACDs 406, 407, and 409 in Toorak—are found in this group, but a few areas have socioeconomic status scores not very much greater than the metropolitan average.

There are two small groups shown in Fig. 7 which require discussion. These again are areas with low ethnicity, but they have somewhat lower socioeconomic status scores than the other groups shown in this figure. Most but not all of these areas comprise Housing Commission estates, a fact which is reflected in the owner-occupancy rates: they average only 62 per cent in these areas, whereas in adjacent ACDs they exceed 90 per cent. But while most of the areas in this group do correspond to the location of estates of the Victorian Housing Commission, there are obviously other areas with public housing not included in this group. Some are to be found in Group 1202, and others in Groups 1201, 1143, 1200, and 1167. However, the areas in Groups 1193 and 1176 shown in this figure tend to have higher socioeconomic status than some other estates, a fact that is partly reflected in their present appearance. One estate, for example, had more trees and better developed gardens than another immediately across a railway line (and in a different local government area). The difference in level of familism between such estates reflects the mixture of housing types, and the relative number of cottages (high familism) compared with walk-up and high rise flats (low familism) (Stevenson, Martin, and O'Neill 1967). Since state housing is not normally available to non-British subjects, it is not surprising that this group is characterised by low ethnicity.

In summarising the discussion of Table 6.2 so far, we can say that all the groups mapped in Fig. 7 are similar to the extent that they tend to be areas of low ethnicity. In fact, except for eleven areas in Groups 1200 and 1167 (again mainly Commission estates), the six groups so far analysed are the only ones the ethnicity scores of which are on average lower than the metropolitan norm. They are also similar in that they all have socioeconomic status scores ranging from slightly above average to very high, except for seven areas in Groups 1193 and 1176. The variation in demographic characteristics is rather more marked, and while most areas are above average in their familism scores, one quite large group is below average. If we were to examine the internal composition of each group more closely, the variability between areas would be much greater than these simplifying averages indicate. But they are still the best groups, in the statistical sense specified above, at this level of social similarity.

To digress for a moment, the reader should remember in interpreting this classification that we are dealing with three dimensions of differentiation simultaneously, in an attempt to construct groups which are internally as homogeneous as possible on all three scales. Considering all these groups together—and they account for 286 of the total number of areas in the study of about 47 per cent of Melbourne's total population in 1961—we find that they are all areas with relatively few non-British settlers. None was in any of the inner city districts, and most lay east and south of the city centre. While some had lower than average socioeconomic status, the majority had above average to high scores on this scale. Only two other groups have as high socioeconomic scores, and these, interestingly enough, are characterised by relatively high ethnicity (Groups 1198 and 1180 discussed below).

Fig. 8 shows the location of eighty-three areas in the eight groups given in the middle section of Table 6.2. As this table indicates, the areas in these groups mostly have low to very low socioeconomic status but high to very high familism. While no relationship was found between socioeconomic status and familism when all the areas in the city were considered together, it is clear from these figures that there are parts of the city where such an association exists. All except a handful of these areas also have higher than average ethnicity scores.

Since the total number of areas in these groups is not large, and since their profiles are not in most cases too dissimilar, it may be simplest to discuss Fig. 8 as a whole. The first and most interesting finding is that these areas fill in most of the missing pieces in the southeast region. The lower socioeconomic status and higher ethnicity of these areas reflect the importance of manufacturing industry in this district (Fig. 3), and the recency of population growth accounts for the high level of familism. The remaining areas in these groups are found north and west of the city, in rapidly developing industrial suburbs on the metropolitan fringe.

To illustrate the social characteristics of areas of this general type, we can take an area from the largest group, ACD 165. Between 1954 and 1961 this area grew rapidly, and in 1961 38 per cent of its population were under fifteen. It had a dependency ratio of 150 dependants for every 100 workers, and less than one in thirty was sixty-five or older. Only 71 per cent were born in Australia, and there were moderately high numbers of new settlers from eastern, central, and southern Europe. In religious characteristics, too, it departed substantially from the Melbourne norm, and there were almost exactly twice as many Catholics as Anglicans (41 and 20 per cent respectively). Seven out of every ten male workers were employed in manufacturing, building and construction, or transport industries, and comparatively few had white-collar or professional jobs. Most of the areas in this group had similar profiles. The reader should remember, however, that the rate of residential development in these western suburbs has gone on apace since 1961, and it will be interesting to see to what extent it has modified the social composition of these new industrial areas.

Figs. 7 and 8, when put together, account for most of the middle distance and fringe suburbs of Melbourne—predominantly Australian-born and middle class east and south (except for some outer areas flanking the Melbourne-Dandenong railway line), and tending towards more immigrant and working class areas north and west. Obviously, Fig. 9 fills in the middle, but before discussing that a final word on Groups 1200 and 1167 is required.

According to Table 6.2 these areas differ from others in this general category by having fewer immigrants. The reason for this is that, as indicated before, these are Housing Commission areas. Groups 1201 and 1143 also overlap with other estates, but their slightly higher ethnicity scores are probably due either to a mixture of public and private housing in the ACDs used in this study, or to the resettlement of some foreign-born persons in outer areas as a result of slum reclamation projects in the inner suburbs. Groups 1201 and 1143 also mainly include state Housing Commission estates.

The capacity of this method of analysis to isolate areas of heavy Housing Commission settlement provides some evidence of its utility. Someone, however, is bound to observe that we could have readily identified such areas without employing the sophisticated techniques adopted in this study. This, like so many criticisms, contains only half the truth. The present study additionally tells us what sort of differences exist between different housing estates and how they differ from other areas in the city. An analysis of how these differences have developed, whether as a direct result of policy decisions or through social processes of a less direct kind, can now be made within the context of a much more rigorous framework. A classification such as that provided here offers a means not simply of identifying different types of social environments but also of analysing the differences between them in a thoroughly systematic and much more enlightening manner.

The final groups shown on Table 6.2 consist of 242 areas, almost all of which are concentrated in a ring of inner suburbs within a six-mile radius of the city centre (Fig. 9). As the average scores for each group indicate, these areas tend to be characterised by high ethnicity and by low familism. They conform to a classic zonal scheme, to what Burgess called the zone in transition—the zone of the boarding houses, flats, rooms, of transients and the unemployed, and of recently arrived immigrant settlers. Perhaps of all the areas in a city, these are marked by extreme social heterogeneity and an intermixture of different social and cultural groups. Some of the areas in these groups have, somewhat unexpectedly, quite high socioeconomic status, a finding which runs contrary to the general relationship between socioeconomic status and ethnicity in the city as a whole. First, however, let us consider the largest group in this section, Group 1196.

As Fig. 9 shows, these areas form an almost continuous belt circling the CBD for a radius of three to four miles. A reasonably typical member of this group is ACD 210. Although even here most of the housing consisted of owner-occupied private houses (60 per cent of all dwellings), the typical house was not a detached cottage but a terrace house dating from some time in the last quarter of the nineteenth century. One in twenty of its male workforce was not at work (mainly unemployed), and only about one in seven of those between fifteen and twenty were still receiving full-time education. Fewer than one in four was a child under fifteen, a figure matched by the percentage of unmarried adults (22 per cent). The dependency ratio was correspondingly low, with 92 dependants for every 100 workers. Only 60 per cent of the total population were native-born, and one in ten was an immigrant who had been in Australia less than four years. Every third person was someone who had been born in Greece, Italy, or Malta, a fact also reflected in its religious composition. Catholics outnumbered Anglicans five to two, and there were twice as many members of the Orthodox churches as Presbyterians.

The next largest group (1174), with 66 areas, formed a narrow band on the edge of this zone of denser ethnic concentration. These are the areas of ecological invasion and succession, into which ethnic groups are spreading as their communities increase in size. As Table 6.2 shows, they have lower ethnicity than areas in Group 1196, but somewhat higher familism and socioeconomic status. A comparison of these two zones poses a number of interesting questions. To what extent does this outer skin represent a zone of secondary settlement among immigrants? Are these areas into which longer established settlers move after an initial period of reorientation, or do they simply represent an overspill as the competition for accommodation in the central areas becomes more intense? Another important area of investigation lies in a comparison of the attitudinal climate of these two zones and the nature of intergroup relationships. Does prejudice increase or decrease among British-Australians as the number of immigrants from non-British countries increases, and what changes, if any, occur in their mutual social relationships? These are questions on which we have little firm evidence. Another interesting fact that emerges from Fig. 9 is that little expansion of these ethnic communities has occurred east of the city, where the River Yarra forms a natural physical barrier. Expansion to the south seems similarly constrained. Do these tendencies reflect the pull of industry and job opportunities to the northern and western sectors of the metropolis, or are other factors at work? Obviously land and property values play a part, but what are the social processes that serve to maintain this division between the predominantly middle class suburbs to the east and south and the mainly working class areas north and west of the city?

So far we have discussed Groups 1196 and 1174 in this last series on Table 6.2. Fig. 6, however, shows three of the remaining groups (1198, 1180, 1185) fuse into a larger group at a higher level in the hierarchy, and we shall consider them together. The areas in these groups tend to be characterised by very low familism. Referring now to Fig. 9, we can see that these areas have a very clear locational pattern. They are concentrated a few miles east of the city centre and to the immediate south of the central business district. They are held apart, as it were, by a thin line of seven ACDs flanking the Yarra and Gardiner's Creek, all of which have very high socioeconomic status. In fact three of these seven interstitial areas (ACDs 406, 407, 209) had the highest socioeconomic status scores in Melbourne, ranking first, second, and fifth highest. These are the areas of the stately homes and Rolls Royces, the traditional location of wealth, power, and prestige in the city for more than a century (Johnston 1966). Much to the regret of many Melbournites, some of these properties have now been subdivided, and large blocks of flats rise up in their place.

Returning to the areas in Groups 1198, 1180, and 1185, we can see that they are all similar in having very low familism. One group, 1185, is less fashionable than the other two and has rather higher ethnicity. By and large these are the areas of high urbanisation, and the many flats and units spread throughout these districts are occupied predominantly by young working adults. Some of these areas were distinctively 'trendy', the areas of boutiques, bright lights, and gay young things. Others had large numbers of university students living in 'digs'. All, as I have said, were characterised by low familism. Without discussing in detail all the areas in these three groups, we can take ACD 511 as an example of some of their main characteristics. Its population had declined by 10 per cent between 1954 and 1961, and one-third of its dwellings consisted of flats. In terms of age structure, it was both old and young. Of every five persons, one was a pensioner or was widowed, one was an unmarried adult, and one a child under fifteen. Its ethnic composition was relatively diverse, and immigrants represented 31 per cent of its total population. Many of them had come from central or eastern Europe, and 7 per cent were Jewish.

Many areas of Jewish concentration are included in Group 1180. There were, of course, other areas with relatively high proportions of Jewish people, but these ACDs had particularly distinctive social profiles. Although in Melbourne as a whole areas of high socioeconomic status usually had few immigrants, these 47 areas had high scores on both these scales. They depart significantly in this respect from other areas in the city. As Fig. 9 shows, these areas extend beyond the zone of densest ethnic concentration, and, unlike them, are located not in the north and west, but in the east and south.

The fact that these areas of Jewish concentration emerge so clearly is extremely interesting, both in itself and also because the ethnicity component did not load heavily on the percentage of Jewish persons in an area. This, it will be remembered, emerged as an independent factor from the general ethnic composition component and was not included directly in this typology (see Table 5.5). This ecological relationship between high socioeconomic status and high ethnicity probably reflects the fact that the collective economic position of Jewish settlers in Melbourne is now more favourable than that of most other ethnic groups, and this rising affluence is reflected in their residential location. It is also likely that economically successful members of southern European groups will follow in the wake of Jewish settlement, as happened in Carlton thirty years ago (Jones 1964). Clearly the identification of this group of areas raises a number of fascinating questions about the social structure of Melbourne, its ethnic and social stratification system, and the general process of social and residential mobility among the members of ethnic minorities.

The very last area to be grouped into our hierarchy was ACD 218, an area with virtually unique characteristics. It had very high ethnicity indeed, and very low familism, combined with very low socioeconomic status. In this area, which was one of the earliest parts of the city to be settled, close to one in five men was 'not at work', and almost all those who were at work were employed in blue-collar jobs. Over half the occupied dwellings were rooms and apartments, and another seventh were boarding houses and the like. Although its total population had declined by over 20 per cent between the two censuses, it had a population density of almost 30,000 persons to the square mile. It was an area of high masculinity and high workforce participation, with two out of every three persons in the workforce, or at least seeking employment. Thirty-seven per cent were unmarried adults. Its ethnic composition was quite diverse. Only half were born in Australia, and of the remainder the greatest proportion were Greek-born (17 per cent). There were more members of the Orthodox churches than there were Anglicans (20 per cent and 18 per cent respectively), and more than one-third were unnaturalised aliens. In terms of its socioeconomic status and ethnicity levels it is not too dissimilar from areas in Group 1196 or some of those shown in Fig. 8, but the combination of these characteristics with such a low level of familism gives it a very distinctive profile.

This completes our discussion of the various types of areas identified in this classification. We could, of course, have structured the discussion in other ways, by taking first one scale and then another. If it was desired to highlight differences in socioeconomic status, attention could have been focused on the two socioeconomic status columns of Table 6.2. This would have led us to include Groups 1198 and 1180 with Groups 1168, 114, and 1197. But by introducing a greater degree of similarity on this one scale we would have increased the diversity along the other dimensions. For some purposes, however, it may be useful to select areas with similar scores along one axis, and to see what variation exists along the others. But in general the simultaneous consideration of all three axes yields more meaningful results. It isolates, for example, different types of Housing Commission estates, and discriminates between ethnic concentrations with different levels of familism and socioeconomic status. It indicates that while most areas with many immigrants from non-British countries of origin have low socioeconomic status, there are other areas where this relationship does not hold. Similarly, it distinguishes systematically between outer industrial and inner industrial areas, and between areas which are similar in terms of socioeconomic status and ethnicity but have different age structures and household composition. By establishing the relative frequency of each different type of area, the classification provides a detailed anatomy of Melbourne's residential structure. Equally important, it establishes a systematic framework for initiating studies designed to fill out and extend the results of this statistical analysis.

Any study of the social and residential structure of a large metropolis gains its fullest value and interpretative meaning when it can be placed in a comparative historical and cultural framework. As detailed studies of Australian cities accumulate, a comprehensive picture of the social differentiation and stratification of urban society in this country will begin to emerge. Although Australia is one of the world's most highly urbanised countries, comparatively little is known about the day-to-day lives its urban residents lead, their hopes and aspirations, their prejudices and practices, or even why they want to live in cities of the Australian mould. A statistical study such as this is not equipped to answer many of these questions. It has, I hope, served to demonstrate the striking diversity of the social environments in which different groups of urban residents find themselves. Anyone who doubts the extent of such diversity need spend only a day travelling from Melbourne's tree-lined eastern suburbs, through the inner industrial areas, across to the industrial suburbs in the west, pausing a little to take in the view, say, from the overpass at Newport railway station. The only features to break the skyline there are the smokestacks, power lines, and grime of industrial activity.

In all modern industrial cities segregation of social groups according to income, life style, and ethnic background occurs. One latent function of this segregation is to shield those who have less from too great and too constant a sense of relative deprivation. It can be stated almost as an axiom that the greater are the economic, social, and ethnic differences between groups, the greater will be the degree of their residential segregation. The existence of such differentials in Australian society have long been de-emphasised. It is not the purpose of this study to over-emphasise them. Obviously Australians enjoy one of the highest and most egalitarian living standards in the world. But there are always two standards to be considered: the absolute standard and the relative standard. Even if most Australians do enjoy high material standards of living, some enjoy them less than others. It is this relative aspect of social differentiation and social stratification that has been the main concern of this study.

By examining the nature of social differences in an Australian metropolis, at least to the extent that they are expressed in a person's choice of a place to live, we have been able to make a number of suggestions about the social and residential structure of Melbourne. Not all of these suggestions could be firmly tested by the information available; some require other forms of inquiry—local surveys, for example. Future studies of this type, however, will not need to rely upon such a wide range of statistical data, and the present analysis provides some guidelines for the choice of salient measures. Perhaps one of the main applications of this method will be in the analysis of social change in urban areas and in studies of social and residential mobility. Social change has, of course, already occurred since the time of the 1961 census, the results of which form the basis of this study. On the rural-urban fringe, where growth is most rapid, and in the inner city areas, where redevelopment—planned and unplanned—is constantly occurring, a considerable degree of social change may have occurred already. Such is the dynamism of a metropolis. Even so, the broad structural features of urban society revealed by these statistics have probably as yet changed little. Precisely how stable this social and physical structure is over time can be established only as a result of future studies.

Social structures are the partly conscious creation of men and women acting in the pursuance of their different needs and interests. The conservative idea that there is something 'natural' or even sacrosanct about the particular social arrangements that prevail at one time or another in a given social structure has long been under challenge by more radical presuppositions. Australia indeed matured into a nation within such a radical tradition, early winning a world-wide reputation for egalitarian reforms. Whether Australia now is less egalitarian than popularly supposed is an open question. Inequalities in life chances certainly exist, as everybody knows. Yet comparisons with the past are difficult to make, if only because social memory is notoriously selective. We choose those ancestors who fit the present need. The others are conveniently forgotten.

The present is best judged on its own merits, in relation to how it measures up to widely held social values. But to make such a judgment implies not only information about those values—that in itself is a substantial problem in a plural society—but also a clearer understanding of the structure of Australian society than we currently possess. The present study represents one step towards that understanding and towards providing a possible basis for social planning. This study is not a study *in* planning, for planning requires the linking of social facts with social values. Depending on their value system some will see nothing in the results of the present study that calls for radical planning. Others may see in residential segregation seeds of potential conflict and may seek for ways to limit its effects. The existence of residentially distinct economic and ethnic groups provides a ready focus for antagonism and prejudice in times of social stress, as is clear from the history of the Great Depression in Australia. Nonetheless, it would be a misreading of the evidence to exaggerate the current importance of such incipient divisions. Compared with other Western democracies Australia is still 'the lucky country' (Horne 1964). Perhaps one result of the sociological endeavour will be to provide an understanding of the social basis for that luck, rather than trust, like a successful gambler, to a permanently lucky streak.

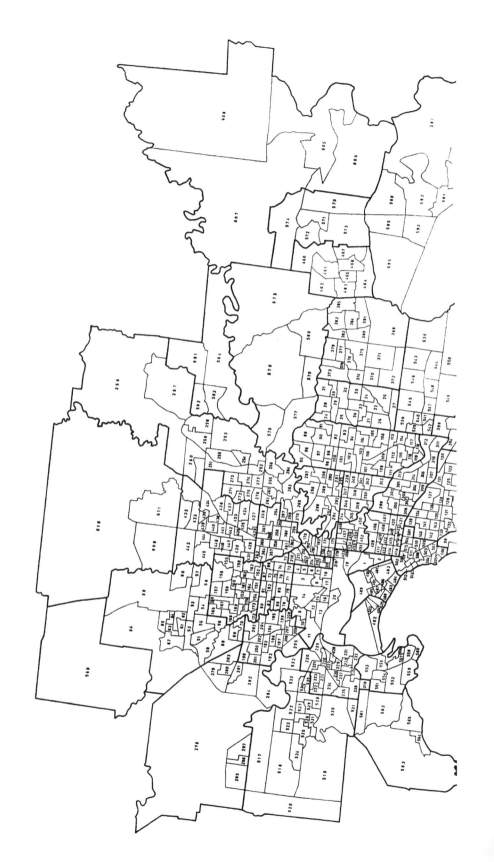

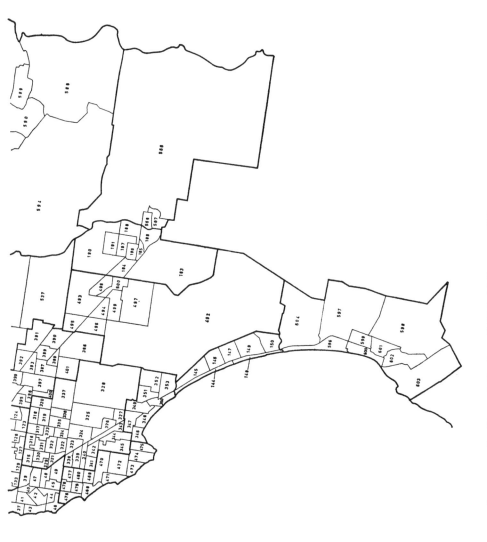

Fig. 10 Base map of aggregated collectors' districts (ACDs), Melbourne, 1961.

Appendix I

Component scores and rank positions on socioeconomic status, familism, and ethnicity for 611 Melbourne ACDs, 1961

Cities, towns, and boroughs	Area	SES score	rank	Familism score	rank	Ethnicity score	rank
City of Melbourne	1	165	555	−323	008	022	361
	2	159	547	−327	007	−068	216
	3	−100	155	−142	103	259	597
	4	−214	036	−145	097	307	607
	5	−078	185	−151	087	267	598
	6	−177	064	−083	214	278	600
	7	−105	149	−163	077	296	604
	8	−087	175	−097	180	106	480
	9	−162	075	−091	198	251	594
	10	−079	181	−091	198	160	535
	11	−186	054	−063	252	162	539
	12	−160	077	−091	198	246	592
	13	−178	061	−069	243	181	561
	14	109	474	−309	010	118	493
	15	−099	158	−170	071	172	549
	16	−141	094	−121	131	227	584
	17	−075	190	−198	051	251	594
	18	−016	263	−294	015	251	594
	19	026	331	−389	003	062	414
	20	−222	033	−137	110	205	575
Box Hill	21	152	535	008	332	−130	093
	22	098	449	−008	314	−135	081
	23	094	440	058	379	−198	018
	24	125	506	089	408	−137	077
	25	029	337	194	546	−100	154
	26	100	456	094	415	−210	010
	27	055	380	196	547	−093	167
	28	103	461	172	519	−081	193
	29	114	489	040	359	−213	009
	30	051	376	164	509	−094	164
	31	036	345	249	587	−027	285
	32	077	416	−049	279	−045	261
	33	073	411	−050	278	−090	174
	34	143	527	228	573	−079	197
	35	170	565	−038	288	−111	120
	36	191	579	−060	261	−141	071

121

Cities, towns, and boroughs	Area	SES score rank		Familism score rank		Ethnicity score rank	
Brighton	37	250	608	−089	205	−065	222
	38	112	482	−129	120	−001	334
	39	165	555	−042	286	−063	227
	40	113	485	−156	081	−009	318
	41	143	527	−126	124	−011	311
	42	171	569	−107	158	−060	233
	43	231	605	−138	108	−081	193
	44	174	571	−053	273	−088	179
	45	205	592	−007	317	−158	048
	46	199	585	−105	164	−066	220
	47	139	522	−007	317	−038	270
	48	147	529	−005	322	−131	090
	49	142	525	099	420	−195	020
Broadmeadows	50	−080	179	270	596	035	381
	51	024	326	168	516	−006	326
	52	−023	256	159	501	071	428
	53	−160	077	205	551	109	483
	54	−131	105	232	578	093	466
	55	−029	244	159	501	082	449
	56	006	295	125	456	−005	329
	57	−206	041	157	498	174	552
	58	−174	067	156	496	075	437
	59	−233	023	193	545	166	545
	60	−241	017	199	548	223	583
	61	−177	064	281	599	−036	271
	62	−194	049	297	605	035	381
	63	−180	059	278	598	033	377
	64	−223	031·	370	609	−018	297
	65	−214	036	306	606	190	563
	66	−120	121	260	592	061	412
	67	−065	197	313	607	−016	300
	68	041	355	167	355	−043	265
	69	125	506	149	485	−136	079
	70	170	565	028	344	−210	010
Brunswick	71	−147	090	−144	099	214	581
	72	−153	084	−084	212	207	578
	73	−177	064	−112	150	196	571
	74	−133	100	−097	180	157	533
	75	−151	086	−149	092	209	580
	76	−221	034	−090	202	201	573
	77	−042	224	−072	233	120	497
	78	044	359	−107	158	053	406
	79	−132	102	−163	077	208	579
	80	−016	263	−091	198	026	369
	81	−092	165	−104	167	141	516

Cities, towns, and boroughs	Area	SES score	rank	Familism score	rank	Ethnicity score	rank
Brunswick (cont.)	82	−170	069	−110	154	176	553
	83	−114	128	−089	205	113	488
	84	−120	121	−067	249	163	542
	85	−197	046	−111	152	230	586
	86	−013	269	−118	139	086	456
	87	−166	073	−107	158	191	565
	88	−092	165	−090	202	144	517
Camberwell	89	196	581	248	586	−086	181
	90	200	587	219	567	−141	071
	91	158	545	215	561	−200	016
	92	197	583	−014	309	−114	110
	93	145	528	−108	156	−112	116
	94	125	506	−099	172	−060	233
	95	247	606	174	523	−099	156
	96	222	602	201	550	−128	095
	97	182	575	128	466	−151	058
	98	171	569	018	337	−108	129
	99	157	544	031	348	−182	026
	100	135	519	−059	264	−065	222
	101	202	588	−122	129	−094	164
	102	193	580	−154	083	−051	249
	103	106	469	−150	089	−006	326
	104	153	536	−076	225	−071	208
	105	166	559	−048	281	−122	100
	106	180	574	−037	290	−142	068
	107	117	494	−153	084	016	355
	108	156	543	−117	142	−085	184
	109	208	594	−097	180	−098	158
	110	202	588	−066	250	−155	052
	111	155	539	−045	284	−110	124
	112	210	596	−023	301	−163	044
	113	155	539	−043	285	−148	063
	114	214	598	108	435	−281	001
	115	211	597	−007	317	−205	013
	116	196	581	−070	238	−181	028
	117	059	389	−007	317	−261	004
	118	−009	276	026	342	−221	007
	119	222	602	099	420	−205	013
Caulfield	120	119	497	−129	120	−105	138
	121	034	343	−122	129	−018	297
	122	081	422	−081	218	−074	205
	123	162	551	079	396	−103	144
	124	111	478	−071	235	−119	105
	125	065	398	−116	144	−062	229
	126	121	499	−037	290	−091	171

Cities, towns, and boroughs	Area	SES score	rank	Familism score	rank	Ethnicity score	rank
Caulfield (cont.)	127	117	494	−060	261	−092	169
	128	127	509	−120	133	−063	227
	129	166	559	−029	297	−039	269
	130	092	438	−203	047	051	401
	131	104	464	−090	202	−048	253
	132	121	499	−134	112	−020	293
	133	136	520	−075	228	−070	210
	134	164	553	−140	105	011	346
	135	178	573	−105	164	003	337
	136	155	539	−114	146	023	362
	137	080	420	−177	065	064	418
	138	114	489	−105	164	014	352
	139	174	571	−149	092	073	432
	140	168	562	−159	080	097	473
	141	219	601	−081	218	047	396
	142	097	446	−181	062	080	445
	143	099	452	−178	063	066	422
Chelsea	144	038	351	−068	247	−149	061
	145	020	321	103	426	−101	150
	146	001	288	053	374	−112	116
	147	−032	238	007	330	−177	033
	148	009	299	−058	265	−100	154
	149	−003	281	078	395	−167	039
	150	−034	236	091	410	−133	087
Coburg	151	−057	206	−127	122	111	485
	152	−045	218	−127	122	093	466
	153	−042	224	−054	271	034	378
	154	002	289	−058	265	025	367
	155	−124	114	−006	320	−031	281
	156	−035	233	033	349	094	469
	157	−048	213	007	330	013	350
	158	−090	168	−012	312	050	398
	159	−030	242	−041	287	−097	160
	160	−056	207	−103	169	098	474
	161	−063	199	−093	193	090	462
	162	−106	145	−056	268	119	495
	163	−002	283	−087	208	064	418
	164	−107	141	−066	250	118	493
	165	−106	145	156	496	114	489
	166	−045	218	093	413	080	445
	167	−030	242	206	553	013	350
	168	005	293	076	394	016	355
	169	028	334	048	367	−006	326
	170	025	329	−069	243	−008	320
	171	077	416	−005	322	−137	077

Cities, towns, and boroughs	Area	SES score rank		Familism score rank		Ethnicity score rank	
Coburg (cont.)	172	004	291	140	480	−058	237
	173	056	383	018	337	−060	233
Collingwood	174	−239	019	−147	096	205	575
	175	−189	051	−148	095	179	557
	176	−226	030	−114	146	112	487
	177	−273	008	−093	193	153	529
	178	−129	107	−177	065	162	539
	179	−168	071	−098	174	160	535
	180	−180	059	−139	107	176	553
	181	−244	015	−109	155	162	539
	182	−291	003	−078	221	228	585
Dandenong	183	−132	102	−115	145	111	485
	184	−125	112	141	482	018	357
	185	−107	141	−094	190	−043	265
	186	−002	283	−014	309	−027	285
	187	−010	274	066	386	−008	320
	188	−025	248	101	424	−081	193
	189	−011	271	−073	231	−002	333
	190	−046	215	209	555	−016	300
	191	−185	055	294	604	−010	315
Essendon	192	084	428	043	361	−103	144
	193	111	478	−062	254	−016	300
	194	−035	233	−097	180	160	535
	195	012	309	−117	142	067	424
	196	−025	248	−186	059	079	442
	197	−060	201	−110	154	108	481
	198	−058	204	−141	104	096	471
	199	080	420	−029	297	−089	177
	200	082	425	−071	235	−068	216
	201	072	408	107	433	−186	024
	202	049	369	−104	167	032	375
	203	097	446	−080	220	−052	247
	204	023	324	−113	148	020	358
	205	−002	283	−069	243	015	354
	206	−100	155	−061	257	151	527
	207	−045	218	−167	074	136	509
	208	−010	274	−132	115	123	499
	209	−089	170	−137	110	−156	050
Fitzroy	210	−140	096	−140	105	197	572
	211	−239	019	−097	180	235	589
	212	−228	028	−076	225	236	590
	213	−195	048	−192	055	233	588
	214	−242	016	−083	214	289	602

Cities, towns, and boroughs	Area	SES score rank		Familism score rank		Ethnicity score rank	
Fitzroy (cont.)	215	−274	006	−124	126	237	591
	216	−253	012	−183	061	285	601
	217	−188	053	−250	025	303	605
	218	−181	057	−414	002	305	606
Footscray	219	−185	055	051	372	096	471
	220	−116	126	−120	133	087	459
	221	−081	178	−144	099	082	449
	222	−091	167	−032	293	−032	279
	223	−078	185	−037	290	009	342
	224	−094	162	−069	243	044	392
	225	−141	094	−113	148	149	524
	226	−116	126	−143	101	146	519
	227	−156	083	−125	125	127	502
	228	−159	079	−068	247	150	525
	229	−122	116	−089	205	115	490
	230	−113	130	−085	210	059	410
	231	−165	074	−133	113	154	531
	232	−158	080	−082	216	144	517
	233	−089	170	001	327	076	440
	234	−142	093	022	340	010	343
	235	−119	123	117	448	083	452
	236	−112	131	−030	296	052	404
	237	−087	175	−031	295	039	386
	238	−126	109	101	424	137	511
Hawthorn	239	108	472	−175	068	035	381
	240	−025	248	−184	060	085	454
	241	−024	252	−150	089	080	445
	242	097	446	−152	086	041	389
	243	217	600	−070	238	−071	208
	244	028	334	−221	038	105	479
	245	065	398	−225	035	067	424
	246	109	474	−229	032	090	462
	247	012	309	−172	069	108	481
	248	043	357	−193	053	071	428
	249	111	478	−259	021	074	434
	250	127	509	−150	089	−006	326
Heidelberg	251	142	525	153	488	−181	028
	252	124	502	028	344	−096	161
	253	113	485	146	484	−032	279
	254	084	428	227	571	−083	187
	255	025	329	211	557	−078	199
	256	048	365	129	468	−046	255
	257	−011	271	159	501	−103	144
	258	064	397	162	505	−098	158

Cities, towns, and boroughs	Area	SES score	rank	Familism score	rank	Ethnicity score	rank
Heidelberg (cont.)	259	033	342	208	554	–203	015
	260	044	359	250	588	–107	132
	261	–060	201	030	347	–080	196
	262	098	449	–049	279	–045	261
	263	167	561	–032	293	–111	120
	264	204	590	063	383	–134	084
	265	171	569	–084	212	–124	098
	266	205	592	060	381	–158	048
	267	–024	252	–006	320	023	362
	268	–025	248	–052	275	038	384
	269	010	302	–070	238	–019	295
	270	008	297	–107	158	062	414
	271	–177	064	229	575	–164	042
	272	–151	086	145	483	–134	084
	273	–126	109	229	575	–166	041
	274	–025	248	066	386	–131	090
	275	–125	112	081	398	–135	081
	276	–135	099	069	388	–240	005
	277	–015	265	–098	174	–114	110
Keilor	278	–059	203	105	430	103	478
	279	–145	091	214	560	131	504
	280	–092	165	127	463	164	543
	281	–055	209	116	446	085	454
	282	010	302	284	600	011	346
	283	031	339	003	328	–107	132
	284	–124	114	216	563	116	491
	285	–255	011	127	463	338	610
	286	–237	022	122	452	317	608
	287	–292	002	219	567	337	609
Kew	288	100	456	–167	074	066	422
	289	076	414	–106	162	039	386
	290	227	604	–096	185	–055	243
	291	150	533	–154	083	043	391
	292	111	478	–189	057	075	437
	293	148	530	–145	097	064	418
	294	170	565	–131	117	073	432
	295	182	575	–130	118	–004	331
	296	169	563	005	329	–021	291
	297	208	594	–061	257	–056	240
	298	155	539	–075	228	–054	245
Malvern	299	285	611	–093	193	–112	116
	300	214	598	–152	086	–061	230
	301	072	408	–214	041	042	390
	302	072	408	–123	127	–012	308

Cities, towns, and boroughs	Area	SES score	rank	Familism score	rank	Ethnicity score	rank
Malvern (cont.)	303	096	442	−160	079	032	375
	304	150	533	−149	092	−027	285
	305	130	515	−118	139	−053	246
	306	154	537	−104	167	−033	277
	307	094	440	−098	174	−034	275
	308	044	359	−202	048	069	426
	309	114	489	−167	074	−016	300
	310	189	578	−052	275	−144	067
	311	129	513	082	399	−153	054
	312	171	569	153	488	−110	124
	313	205	592	−085	210	−084	186
	314	254	609	−096	185	−057	239
Moorabbin	315	167	561	−051	277	−090	174
	316	116	493	−034	292	−146	065
	317	124	502	187	543	−101	150
	318	032	341	154	490	−060	233
	319	069	403	257	590	−035	272
	320	049	369	182	536	−112	116
	321	111	478	020	339	−114	110
	322	119	497	126	459	−074	205
	323	128	511	126	459	−021	291
	324	061	392	161	503	−012	308
	325	068	402	178	529	−014	305
	326	−014	267	172	519	−085	184
	327	082	425	155	493	−101	150
	328	050	373	166	513	−069	213
	329	113	485	−006	320	−086	181
	330	099	452	−060	261	−070	210
	331	125	506	−046	283	−113	113
	332	123	501	045	364	−111	120
	333	082	425	086	404	−106	135
	334	070	404	216	563	−074	205
	335	030	338	223	569	−034	275
	336	048	365	210	556	−012	308
	337	011	305	185	539	−064	224
	338	018	317	024	341	−102	146
	339	006	295	043	361	−139	073
	340	005	293	055	377	−147	064
	341	056	383	176	527	−200	016
	342	074	412	085	402	−105	138
	343	108	472	075	392	−198	018
	344	113	485	123	453	−167	039
	345	105	466	227	571	−172	035
Mordialloc	346	128	511	091	410	−154	053
	347	119	497	−018	305	−101	150

Cities, towns, and boroughs	Area	SES score	rank	Familism score	rank	Ethnicity score	rank
Mordialloc (cont.)	348	106	469	–097	180	–071	208
	349	104	464	014	336	–141	071
	350	049	369	–063	252	–104	140
	351	056	383	170	517	–133	087
	352	–020	258	180	533	–101	150
	353	020	321	–017	306	–069	213
Northcote	354	–024	252	050	370	045	394
	355	–089	170	–061	257	012	348
	356	–101	152	–093	193	079	442
	357	–012	270	–069	243	074	434
	358	–131	105	–101	170	090	462
	359	–098	160	–076	225	066	422
	360	–035	233	–119	136	073	432
	361	–128	108	–097	180	140	515
	362	–121	118	–119	136	124	500
	363	–024	252	–070	238	–007	323
	364	–066	196	–076	225	024	365
	365	–053	210	–106	162	077	441
	366	–060	201	–111	152	102	476
	367	–045	218	–087	208	025	367
	368	–040	226	050	370	–014	305
Nunawading	369	093	439	230	577	–077	200
	370	081	422	218	565	–138	074
	371	057	387	265	595	–106	135
	372	059	389	205	551	–059	236
	373	104	464	119	450	–046	255
	374	165	555	155	493	–190	022
	375	099	452	154	490	–108	129
	376	115	491	038	357	–151	058
	377	059	389	180	533	–129	094
	378	070	404	172	519	–082	189
	379	051	376	259	591	–039	269
	380	056	383	226	570	–112	116
	381	051	376	138	478	–107	132
	382	056	383	172	519	–089	177
	383	061	392	063	383	–093	167
	384	061	392	137	476	–090	174
	385	018	317	165	511	–068	216
Oakleigh	386	–106	145	139	479	047	396
	387	–111	133	121	451	034	378
	388	–039	228	100	422	006	340
	389	–034	236	115	445	–028	283
	390	–106	145	164	509	040	388
	391	–056	207	164	509	–041	267

Cities, towns, and boroughs	Area	SES score rank		Familism score rank		Ethnicity score rank	
Oakleigh (cont.)	392	022	323	180	533	−004	331
	393	−078	185	124	454	003	337
	394	036	345	−098	174	011	346
	395	011	305	−072	233	−024	288
	396	047	362	−024	300	−077	200
	397	014	313	099	420	−068	216
	398	048	365	105	430	−050	251
	399	−019	259	−013	311	−014	305
	400	031	339	096	416	−081	193
	401	−048	213	165	511	036	383
Port Melbourne	402	−178	061	−118	139	007	341
	403	−231	025	−095	187	075	437
	404	−176	066	−132	115	135	507
	405	−162	075	−096	185	063	416
Prahran	406	247	606	−168	072	−008	320
	407	281	610	−143	101	−015	303
	408	132	517	−230	030	058	409
	409	159	547	−310	009	024	365
	410	004	291	−281	017	138	513
	411	−013	269	−258	023	131	504
	412	−076	188	−223	037	138	513
	413	−133	100	−210	043	177	555
	414	−044	222	−281	017	133	506
	415	−111	133	−193	053	146	519
	416	−040	226	−235	028	135	507
	417	−035	233	−218	039	191	565
	418	028	334	−281	017	124	500
	419	−045	218	−186	059	138	513
	420	071	406	−234	029	051	401
	421	097	446	−301	012	065	420
	422	068	402	−244	027	086	456
Preston	423	−006	279	048	367	−028	283
	424	−191	050	128	466	−033	277
	425	−044	222	−023	301	−016	300
	426	−037	230	−081	218	030	373
	427	−058	204	011	334	−011	311
	428	−106	145	−095	187	062	414
	429	−067	194	−076	225	−019	295
	430	038	351	−052	275	−023	289
	431	039	354	−016	307	−082	189
	432	−170	069	241	583	052	404
	433	−076	188	200	549	−034	275
	434	−120	121	211	557	−011	311
	435	−199	044	173	522	−127	096

Cities, towns, and boroughs	Area	SES score	rank	Familism score	rank	Ethnicity score	rank
Preston (cont.)	436	−131	105	133	473	−100	154
	437	−238	021	235	580	−085	184
	438	−023	256	131	469	−163	044
	439	−079	181	034	350	−135	081
	440	046	361	037	354	−076	202
	441	008	297	−054	271	−010	315
	442	−018	260	−061	257	−020	293
	443	−138	098	217	564	057	408
	444	−017	261	036	353	−045	261
	445	−049	212	163	507	−046	255
	446	−050	211	054	376	−082	189
	447	038	351	−020	303	−045	261
	448	−031	239	128	466	−056	240
Richmond	449	−227	029	−116	144	120	497
	450	−151	086	−094	190	153	529
	451	−231	025	−133	113	173	551
	452	−233	023	−122	129	162	539
	453	−150	088	−226	034	206	577
	454	−121	118	−215	040	217	582
	455	−197	046	−200	050	232	587
	456	−205	043	−088	207	169	547
	457	−189	051	−072	233	194	569
	458	−168	071	−129	120	193	567
	459	−157	081	−211	042	194	569
Ringwood	460	080	420	181	535	−151	058
	461	101	458	106	432	−079	197
	462	079	418	157	498	−055	243
	463	061	392	149	485	−103	144
	464	097	446	175	525	−152	055
	465	106	469	096	416	−164	042
	466	096	442	179	530	−064	224
	467	111	478	188	544	−121	102
Sandringham	468	105	466	−149	092	−052	247
	469	076	414	−055	269	−138	074
	470	159	547	−019	304	−175	034
	471	086	430	−078	221	−075	203
	472	164	553	044	363	−167	039
	473	129	513	062	382	−159	047
	474	184	577	256	589	−214	008
	475	197	583	239	581	−192	021
	476	152	535	−094	190	−045	261
	477	036	345	012	335	−181	028
	478	132	517	−060	261	−142	068
	479	103	461	−120	133	−125	097
	480	048	365	−004	325	−156	050

Cities, towns, and boroughs	Area	SES score	rank	Familism score	rank	Ethnicity score	rank
South Melbourne	481	161	550	−427	001	−008	320
	482	−031	239	−258	023	076	440
	483	−030	242	−250	025	090	462
	484	013	311	−266	020	091	465
	485	−209	039	−137	110	196	571
	486	−110	136	−119	136	099	475
	487	−105	149	−303	011	148	522
	488	−067	194	−230	030	094	469
	489	−068	191	−165	076	094	469
	490	−118	124	−177	065	154	531
	491	−122	116	−192	055	180	559
Springvale	492	−005	280	111	440	−055	243
	493	−112	131	105	430	038	384
	494	−100	155	114	444	021	360
	495	−110	136	118	449	050	398
	496	−099	158	070	390	084	453
	497	−116	126	124	454	087	459
	498	−108	138	127	463	−010	315
	499	−098	160	133	473	−006	326
	500	−045	218	109	438	−010	315
St Kilda	501	138	521	−202	048	102	476
	502	028	334	−353	005	120	497
	503	092	438	−223	037	166	545
	504	072	408	−228	033	148	522
	505	159	547	−196	052	087	459
	506	132	517	−207	046	073	432
	507	090	434	−171	070	−133	087
	508	047	362	−271	019	165	544
	509	090	434	−177	065	127	502
	510	037	348	−208	045	160	535
	511	−014	267	−210	043	118	493
	512	−002	283	−365	004	151	527
	513	024	326	−301	012	179	557
	514	100	456	−258	023	148	522
	515	019	319	−295	014	150	525
	516	−015	265	−348	006	173	551
Sunshine	517	−274	006	108	435	359	611
	518	−230	027	162	505	251	594
	519	−265	010	174	523	290	603
	520	−281	004	126	459	069	426
	521	−206	041	052	373	203	574
	522	−210	038	136	475	191	565
	523	−211	037	132	471	170	548
	524	−207	040	070	390	181	561

Cities, towns, and boroughs	Area	SES score	rank	Familism score	rank	Ethnicity score	rank
Sunshine (cont.)	525	−110	136	−004	325	012	348
	526	−093	163	093	413	027	370
	527	−249	013	088	406	110	484
	528	−223	031	116	446	−171	036
	529	−241	017	080	397	−091	171
	530	−156	083	059	380	027	370
	531	−103	151	026	342	053	406
	532	−038	229	−010	313	030	373
	533	−085	177	075	392	−097	160
	534	−198	045	037	354	−094	164
	535	−139	097	−014	309	−045	261
Waverley	536	086	430	284	600	−150	060
	537	−064	198	176	527	028	372
	538	050	373	186	541	−093	167
	539	−023	256	126	459	−120	103
	540	−088	173	140	480	−264	003
	541	−088	173	166	513	−277	002
	542	−105	149	229	575	−209	012
	543	099	452	271	597	−090	174
	544	074	412	262	594	−102	146
	545	125	506	290	602	−131	090
	546	089	432	260	592	−134	084
	547	102	460	290	602	−131	090
	548	149	531	323	608	−181	028
	549	041	355	240	582	−044	264
	550	141	523	184	538	−060	233
Williamstown	551	−171	068	053	374	178	556
	552	−125	112	034	350	020	358
	553	−114	128	−027	299	024	365
	554	−079	181	−074	230	044	392
	555	−101	152	−091	198	082	449
	556	−108	138	−061	257	051	401
	557	−088	173	−048	281	014	352
	558	−068	191	−068	247	061	412
	559	050	373	−057	267	−111	120
	560	−098	160	−101	170	055	407

Shires	Area	SES score	rank	Familism score	rank	Ethnicity score	rank
Altona	561	−272	009	187	543	189	562
	562	−361	001	156	496	273	599
	563	−144	092	177	528	082	449
	564	−079	181	038	357	000	335
	565	−076	188	038	357	005	339
Berwick (part)	566	016	314	093	413	−069	213
	567	−280	005	405	610	010	343
	568	−249	013	440	611	046	395
Bulla (part)	569	056	383	104	428	−180	031
Croydon	570	038	351	113	442	−122	100
	571	027	332	086	404	−168	037
	572	112	482	085	402	−178	032
	573	000	287	161	503	−082	189
	574	052	378	108	435	−118	106
Doncaster and Templestowe	575	049	369	131	469	−105	138
	576	115	491	233	579	−063	227
	577	066	400	244	584	−026	287
	578	165	555	155	493	−161	046
	579	090	434	213	559	−058	237
	580	086	430	218	565	−046	255
Eltham (part)	581	010	302	089	408	−114	110
	582	012	309	113	442	−120	103
	583	024	326	180	533	−152	055
	584	090	434	110	439	−117	107
Fern Tree Gully (part)	585	−007	278	112	441	−110	124
	586	009	299	091	410	−183	025
	587	101	458	057	378	−137	077
	588	000	287	074	391	−122	100
	589	018	317	010	333	−106	135
	590	011	305	029	346	−110	124
	591	037	348	083	400	−066	220
	592	014	313	049	369	−114	110
	593	017	315	101	424	−051	249
	594	011	305	186	541	−034	275
	595	009	299	137	476	−010	315
Frankston	596	062	395	048	367	−148	063
	597	−010	274	247	585	−094	164
	598	063	396	132	471	−067	219
	599	025	329	−004	325	000	335
	600	108	472	−055	269	−088	179

Shires	Area	SES		Familism		Ethnicity	
		score	rank	score	rank	score	rank
Frankston (cont.)	601	036	345	046	365	−045	066
	602	156	543	150	487	−224	006
	603	199	585	066	386	−189	023
	604	−035	233	109	438	−109	127
Lillydale (part)	605	−067	194	126	459	−104	140
	606	019	319	042	360	−092	169
	607	054	379	085	402	−109	127
	608	−008	277	035	352	−050	251
Whittlesea (part)	609	−107	141	103	426	136	509
	610	−028	245	097	418	−005	329
	611	−149	089	183	537	082	449

Appendix II

A key to the composition of named localities in the Melbourne metropolitan area*

Postal district and postcode		Constituent ACDs					
Abbotsford	3067	174	175	182†			
Albert Park	3206	483	484	486†	487	488	
Alphington	3078	267†	268†	269	270†	354†	
Altona	3018	563	564	565			
Armadale	3143	300†	308	420†	421		
Ascot Vale	3032	205	206	207	208	209	
Ashburton	3147	113†	114†	116	117	118	119†
		538†	539	540			
Aspendale	3195	145					
Balaclava	3183	140	501	509	510	514	
Balwyn	3103	90†	91†	92	94†	98†	99
		100	101				
Balwyn North	3104	89	90†	91†	95	96	97
		98†					
Beaumaris	3193	344†	345†	346†	472†	473†	474
		475					
Bentleigh	3204	315	316	321†	329	330	331
		332	333†				
Bentleigh East	3165	317	318	319	333†	334	335
		336					
Black Rock	3193	471†	472†	473†			
Box Hill	3128	22†	23	24	25	29†	32
		33					
Box Hill North	3129	28	29†	30	31	34	
Braybrook	3019	522†	527	528	529	530†	
Brighton	3186	37†	40	41	42†	43	44
		46					
Brighton East	3187	39	45	47	48	49	
Brunswick	3056	71	73	75	76	79	81
		82	83†	84†	85	87	
Brunswick East	3057	72	74	77	88		
Brunswick West	3055	78	80	83†	84†	86	
Burwood	3125	26	27†	106†	112†	113†	114†
		115†	538†				
Camberwell	3124	103†	104†	105†	106†	107†	108
		109	110†	240†			
Canterbury	3126	94†	102	103†	104†	107†	110†
Carlton	3053	6†	7	8	17	18	
Carlton North	3054	3	4	5	6†		

Postal district and postcode		Constituent ACDs					
Carnegie	3163	121	125	126	127	137†	
Caulfield	3162	128	129	131	133	135	136†
		138					
Caulfield North	3161	134	136†	137†	139	141	309†
Chadstone	3148	311	312†	398	541	542	
Chelsea	3196	144†	147	148†	149†		
Cheltenham	3192	325†	326†	327	343†	344†	345†
		470†	472†				
Clifton Hill	3068	179	180	181†			
Coburg	3058	151	152	153	154	158†	159
		160	161	162	163	164	
Coburg North	3058	155	156	157	158†		
Collingwood	3066	176	177	178	181†	182†	
East Melbourne	3002	19					
Edithvale	3196	144†	146				
Elsternwick	3185	38†	42	130	132	142	143
Elwood	3184	38†	503	504†	505	506	507
Essendon	3040	192†	193	199	200	201	202
		203	204				
Essendon North	3041	50	68	69	70	283	
Fairfield	3078	267†	268†	270†	354†		
Fawkner	3060	57	58†	60			
Fitzroy	3065	215	216	217	218		
Fitzroy North	3068	210	211	212	213	214	
Flemington	3031	9†	10	11	12†		
Footscray	3011	220	221		223†	225	226
		227	228	229†	231†		
Footscray West	3012	222	223†	224	234	235†	236
		237†					
Glen Iris	3146	111	112†	115†	119†	243†	303†
		305	313†	314†			
Glenroy	3046	52†	53	54†	55†	58†	61
		62†					
Hampton	3188	476	477	478	479	480	
Hawthorn	3122	244	245	246	247	248	249
		250					
Hawthorn East	3123	239	240†	241	242	243†	
Heidelberg	3084	251†	252	253	254	255†	266
Heidelberg West	3081	271	272	273	274	275	276
		277					
Highett	3190	324†	326†	340	341†	342	343†
Ivanhoe	3079	261	262	263	264	265	
Keon Park	3073	432†	443				
Kew	3101	288	289	291†	292	293	294
		295†	296				
Kew East	3102	290	291†	295†	297	298	
Maidstone	3012	532†	533†	534	535		
Malvern	3144	299†	300†	301	302	303†	309†

K

Postal district and postcode		Constituent ACDs					
Malvern East	3145	119†	304	306	307	309†	310
		312†	313†	314†			
Maribyrnong	3032	532†					
Mentone	3194	346†	347	348	349		
Moonee Ponds	3039	192†	194	195	196	197	198
Moorabbin	3189	321†	322	323	324†	338	339
Mordialloc	3195	350	351	352	353		
Murrumbeena	3163	120	122	123	124		
Newport	3015	551	552†	554	555	562†	
Northcote	3070	355	356	357	358	359	360
		361	362				
North Melbourne	3051	12†	13	15	16		
Oakleigh	3166	393†	394	395	396	397†	399
Oakleigh South	3167	320	337†	387†	397†	400	
Parkville	3052	9†	14				
Pascoe Vale	3044	54†	55†	56	165	166	167
		168	169†				
Pascoe Vale South	3044	169†	170†	171	172	173	
Port Melbourne	3207	402†	403	404	405		
Port Melbourne West	3207	402†					
Prahran	3181	414	415	416	417	418	419
		420†	422				
Preston	3072	423	424	425	426	427	428
		429	430	431	437†	442	447†
Reservoir	3073	432†	433	434†	435	436	437†
		438	439	440	441	444	445
		446	447†	448†			
Richmond	3121	449	450	451	452	453	454
		455	456	457	458	459	
St Kilda	3182	502†	504†	508	511	512	513
		515	516				
Sandringham	3191	468	469	470†	471†		
South Melbourne	3205	485	486†	489	490	491	
South Yarra	3141	1	2	409	410	411	412
		413					
Spotswood	3015	219	238	553†	561		
Sunshine	3020	522†	523	525	526	530†	531
Surrey Hills	3127	21	22†	35	36	93	104†
		105†					
Thornbury	3071	354†	363	364	365	366	367
		368					
Toorak	3142	299†	406	407	408		
Williamstown	3016	556	557	558	559†	560	
Williamstown West	3016	552†	559†				
Yarraville	3013	229†	230	231†	232	233	235†
		237†	238†				

Postal district and postcode		Constituent ACDs					
Outer suburbs							
Ardeer, Deer Park	3022-3	519	520				
Blackburn	3130	373	374	375†	376	377†	378
		379					
Burwood East	3151	371†	372				
Campbellfield	3061	59					
Carrum	3197	148†	149†	150			
Clarinda	3169	337†	341†	401			
Clayton	3168	388	389	390			
Croydon	3136	570	571	572	573		
Croydon North	3136	574					
Dandenong	3175	184	185	186	187	188	189
		190	191				
Doncaster, Templestowe	3108-6	577†	578	579	580		
Doveton	3177	566†	567	568			
Eltham	3095	581	584†				
Epping	3076	610					
Forest Hill	3131	370	371†				
Frankston	3199	596†	597	599	600		
Glen Waverley	3150	536	543	544			
Keilor	3036	278					
Macleod	3085	251†	255†				
Mitcham	3132	381	383	384	385		
Montmorency	3094	582	583				
Mt Waverley	3149	545	546	547	548		
Niddrie	3042	279†	280	281†	282†		
Noble Park	3174	498	500				
Notting Hill	3168	391	392	393†	549		
Nunawading	3131	375†	377†	380	382		
Ringwood	3134	460	461	462	463	464	465
		466	467				
St Albans	3021	285	286	287	517		
Springvale	3171	386†	493	494	495	496	499
Springvale South	3170	497					
Thomastown, Lalor	3074-5	609	611				
Vermont	3133	369					
Watsonia, Greensborough	3087-8	259	260				

* Boundaries and locations of these districts were derived from *Sands and MacDougall's Street Directory*, Melbourne, 1965. Districts the boundaries of which could not be established with relative accuracy have been excluded (Jones 1967d). The scores given in the appendix to Jones 1967d are expressed in a different scale from those given in this appendix.

† Part only.

References

Adler, Dan L. and Taft, Ronald (1966). 'Some psychological aspects of immigrant assimilation', in Alan Stoller (ed.), *New Faces: Immigration and Family Life in Australia*, Melbourne, F. W. Cheshire.

Anderson, Theodore R. and Egeland, Janice A. (1961). 'Spatial aspects of social area analysis', *American Sociological Review*, 26 (June): 392-8.

Arsdol, Maurice van, jun., Camilleri, Santo F., and Schmid, Calvin F. (1961). 'An investigation of the utility of urban typology', *Pacific Sociological Review*, 4 (Spring) : 26-32.

——, ——, and —— (1962). 'Further comments on the utility of urban typology', *Pacific Sociological Review*, 5 (Spring) : 1-13.

Bell, Wendell (1965). 'Urban neighborhood and individual behavior', in Muzafer and Carolyn W. Sherif (eds.), *Problems of Youth: Transition to Adulthood in a Changing World*, Chicago, Aldine Publishing Co.

—— and Moskos, Charles C., jun. (1964). 'A comment on Udry's "increasing scale and spatial differentiation"', *Social Forces*, 42 (May) : 414-17.

Beshers, James M. (1962). *Urban Social Structure*, New York, Free Press of Glencoe.

Brennan, T. (1963). 'The pattern of urbanization in Australia', *International Journal of Comparative Sociology*, 4 (September): 152-61.

Briggs, Asa (1963). *Victorian Cities*, London, Odhams Press.

Burgess, Ernest W. (1925). 'The growth of the city: an introduction to a research project', in Robert E. Park, Ernest W. Burgess, and Roderick D. McKenzie (eds.) , *The City*, Chicago, University of Chicago Press.

—— (ed.) (1926). *The Urban Community*, Chicago, University of Chicago Press.

Butlin, N. G. (1964). *Investment in Australian Economic Development 1861-1900*, Cambridge, Cambridge University Press.

141

Campbell, W. J. (1963). *Growing Up in Karribee*, Melbourne, Australian Council for Educational Research.

Cartwright, Desmond S. (1965). 'A misapplication of factor analysis', *American Sociological Review*, **30** (April): 249-51.

Chaddock, Robert E. (1934). 'Significance of infant mortality rates for small geographic areas', *Journal of the American Statistical Association*, **29** (September): 243-9.

Connell, W. F., Francis, E. P., and Skilbeck, E. E. (1957). *Growing Up in an Australian City*, Melbourne, Australian Council for Educational Research.

Day, Lincoln H. (1965). 'Family size and fertility', in A. F. Davies and S. Encel (eds.), *Australian Society: A Sociological Introduction*, Melbourne, F. W. Cheshire.

Duncan, Otis Dudley and Duncan, Beverly (1955). 'Residential distribution and occupational stratification', *American Journal of Sociology*, **60** (March): 493-503.

Elkin, A. P. (ed.) (1957). *Marriage and the Family in Australia*, Sydney, Angus and Robertson.

Farrag, Abdelmegid M. (1964). 'The occupational structure of the labour force: patterns and trends in selected countries', *Population Studies*, **18** (July): 17-34.

Finn, E. ('Garryowen') (1888). *The Chronicles of Early Melbourne 1835 to 1852: Historical, Anecdotal and Personal*, Melbourne, Fergusson and Mitchell, 2 vols.

Garrison, L. G. *et al.* (1959). *Studies in Highway Development and Geographic Change*, Seattle, University of Washington Press.

Grant, James and Serle, Geoffrey (1957). *The Melbourne Scene 1803-1956*, Melbourne, Melbourne University Press.

Hadden, Jeffrey K. and Borgatta, Edgar F. (1965). *American Cities: Their Social Characteristics*, Chicago, Rand McNally.

Hall, W. H. (1905). *Statistics: Six States of Australia and New Zealand, 1861-1904*, Sydney, Government Printer.

Harman, Harry H. (1960). *Modern Factor Analysis*, Chicago, University of Chicago Press.

Hatt, Paul (1946). 'The concept of the natural area', *American Sociological Review*, **11** (August): 423-7.

Hauser, Philip M. (1956). 'Ecological aspects of urban reseach', in L. D. White (ed.), *The State of the Social Sciences*, Chicago, University of Chicago Press.

Hawley, Amos H. and Duncan, Otis Dudley (1957). 'Social area analysis: a critical appraisal', *Land Economics*, **33** (November): 337-45.

Hollingshead, August B. and Redlich, Frederick C. (1958). *Social Class and Mental Illness: A Community Study*, New York, John Wiley and Sons.

Horne, Donald (1964). *The Lucky Country*, Melbourne, Penguin Books.

Hoyt, Homer (1939). *The Structure and Growth of Residential Neighborhoods in American Cities*, Washington D.C., U.S. Government Printing Office.

Johnston, R. J. (1966). 'The location of high status residential areas', *Geografiska Annaler*, 48 (Ser. B): 23-35.

Jones, F. Lancaster (1964). 'Italians in the Carlton area: the growth of an ethnic concentration', *Australian Journal of Politics and History*, 10 (April): 83-95.

—— (1965). 'A social profile of Canberra, 1961', *Australian and New Zealand Journal of Sociology*, 1 (October): 107-20.

—— (1967a). 'Australia's changing occupational structure', *Hemisphere*, 11 (February): 2-6.

—— (1967b). 'Ethnic concentration and assimilation: an Australian case study', *Social Forces*, 45 (March): 412-23.

—— (1967c). 'A social ranking of Melbourne suburbs', *Australian and New Zealand Journal of Sociology*, 3 (October): 93-110.

—— (1968). 'Social area analysis: some theoretical and methodological comments illustrated with Australian data', *British Journal of Sociology*, 19 (December): 424-44.

Kendall, M. G. (1957). *A Course in Multivariate Statistics*, London, Charles Griffin.

Kendall, Patricia L. and Lazarsfeld, Paul F. (1955). 'The relation between individual and group characteristics in "The American Soldier" ', in Paul F. Lazarsfeld and Morris Rosenberg (eds.), *The Language of Social Research*, New York, Free Press of Glencoe.

Lieberson, Stanley (1963). *Ethnic Patterns in American Cities*, New York, Free Press of Glencoe.

Linge, G. J. R. (1962). 'The location of manufacturing in Australia', in Alex Hunter (ed.), *The Economics of Australian Industry*, Melbourne, Melbourne University Press.

—— (1965). *The Delimitation of Urban Boundaries for Statistical Purposes with Special Reference to Australia*, Canberra, Australian National University Press.

McElrath, Dennis L. (1962). 'The social areas of Rome: a comparative analysis', *American Sociological Review*, 27 (June): 376-91.

McElrath, Dennis L. (1968). 'Societal scale and social differentiation: Accra, Ghana,' in Scott Greer *et al.* (eds.), *The New Urbanization*, New York, St Martin's Press.

Martin, Jean I. (1967). 'Extended kinship ties: an Adelaide study', *Australian and New Zealand Journal of Sociology*, 3 (April): 44-63.

Melbourne and Metropolitan Board of Works (1954). *Melbourne Metropolitan Planning Scheme 1954: Surveys and Analysis*, Melbourne, McLaren and Co.

—— (1967). *The Future Growth of Melbourne*, Melbourne, Port Phillip Press.

Menzel, Herbert (1950). 'Comment on Robinson's "Ecological correlations and the behavior of individuals" ', *American Sociological Review*, 15 (October): 674.

Moser, C. A. and Scott, Wolf (1961). *British Towns: A Statistical Study of Their Social and Economic Differences*, Edinburgh and London, Oliver and Boyd.

Nadel, S. F. (1953). *The Foundations of Social Anthropology*, London, Cohen and West Ltd.

Oeser, O. A. and Emery, F. E. (eds.) (1954). *Social Structure and Personality in a Rural Community*, London, Routledge and Kegan Paul.

—— and Hammond, S. B. (eds.) (1954). *Social Structure and Personality in a City*, London, Routledge and Kegan Paul.

Park, Robert E. (1952). *Human Communities: The City and Human Ecology*, New York, Free Press of Glencoe.

Porter, John (1965). *The Vertical Mosaic: An Analysis of Social Class and Power in Canada*, Toronto, University of Toronto Press.

Price, C. A. (1957). 'The effects of post-war immigration on the growth of population, ethnic composition, and religious structure of Australia', *Australian Quarterly*, 29 (December): 28-40.

Robinson, K. W. (1962). 'Process and patterns of urbanization in Australia and New Zealand', *New Zealand Geographer*, 18 (April): 32-49.

Robinson, W. J. (1950). 'Ecological correlations and the behavior of individuals', *American Sociological Review*, 15 (June): 351-7.

Ross, Frank Alexander (1933). 'Ecology and the statistical method', *American Journal of Sociology*, 38 (January): 507-22.

Rossi, Peter H. (1955). *Why Families Move: A Study in the Social Psychology of Urban Residential Mobility*, New York, Free Press of Glencoe.

Schmid, Calvin F. (1938). 'The theory and practice of planning census tracts', *Sociology and Social Research*, 22 (January-February): 228-38.

— (1960a). 'Urban crime areas: Part I', *American Sociological Review*, 25 (August): 527-42.

— (1960b). 'Urban crime areas: Part II', *American Sociological Review*, 25 (October): 655-78.

— and Tagashira, Kiyoshi (1964). 'Ecological and demographic indices: a methodological analysis', *Demography*, 1: 194-211.

Scott, Peter (1965). 'The population structure of Australian cities', *The Geographical Journal*, 131 (December): 463-78.

Seal, Hilary L. (1964). *Multivariate Statistical Analysis for Biologists*, London, Methuen.

Shevky, Eshref and Bell, Wendell (1955). *Social Area Analysis: Theory, Illustrative Application, and Computational Procedures*, Stanford, Stanford University Press.

— and Williams, Marilyn (1949). *The Social Areas of Los Angeles: Analysis and Typology*, Berkeley, University of California Press.

Simmel, George (1902). 'The number of members as determining the sociological form of the group', *American Journal of Sociology*, 8 (July): 1-46; (September): 158-96.

Sinclair, W. A. (1964). 'Industrial distribution of the Melbourne workforce since 1871', paper presented to the Social Science Research Council Conference on the Metropolis in Australia (mimeo.).

Smith, J. (ed.) (1903). *The Cyclopedia of Victoria*, Melbourne, F. W. Niven & Co., 2 vols.

Stevenson, Anne, Martin, Elaine, and O'Neill, Judith (1967). *High Living: A Study of Family Life in Flats*, Melbourne, Melbourne University Press.

Sweetser, Frank L. (1962). *The Social Ecology of Metropolitan Boston*, Division of Mental Hygiene, Massachusetts Department of Mental Health.

— (1965). 'Factorial ecology: Helsinki, 1960', *Demography*, 2: 372-85.

Taeuber, Karl E. and Taeuber, Alma F. (1965). *Negroes in Cities: Residential Segregation and Neighborhood Change*, Chicago, Aldine Publishing Co.

Theodorson, George A. (ed.) (1961). *Studies in Human Ecology*, Illinois and New York, Row, Peterson and Co.

Tryon, Robert C. (1955). *Identification of Social Areas by Cluster Analysis: A General Method with an Application to the San Francisco Bay Area*, Berkeley and Los Angeles, University of California Press.

Twopeny, R. E. N. (1883). *Town Life in Australia*, London, Stock.

Udry, J. Richard (1964). 'Increasing scale and spatial differentiation: new tests of two theories from Shevky and Bell', *Social Forces*, 42 (May): 403-13.

U.S. Bureau of the Census (1961). *1960 Census of the Population*, 1: xviii-xxviii.

Warner, W. Lloyd, Meeker, Marchia, and Eells, Kenneth (1949). *Social Class in America: A Manual of Procedure for the Measurement of Social Status*, Chicago, Science Research Associates, Inc.

Williams, W. T. and Lance, G. N. (1965). 'Logic of computer-based intrinsic classifications', *Nature*, 207 (July): 159-61.

Wilson, Godfrey and Wilson, Monica (1954). *The Analysis of Social Change Based on Observations in Central Africa*, Cambridge, Cambridge University Press.

Wirth, Louis (1938). 'Urbanism as a way of life', *American Journal of Sociology*, 44 (July): 1-24.

Zorbaugh, Harvey W. (1926). 'The natural areas of the city', in Ernest W. Burgess (ed.), *The Urban Community*, Chicago, University of Chicago Press.

Zubrzycki, Jerzy (1960). *Immigrants in Australia: A Demographic Survey Based on the 1954 Census*, Melbourne, Melbourne University Press.

—— (1964). *Settlers of the Latrobe Valley*, Canberra, Australian National University.

Index

Text set in 10 pt Linotype Baskerville,
two points

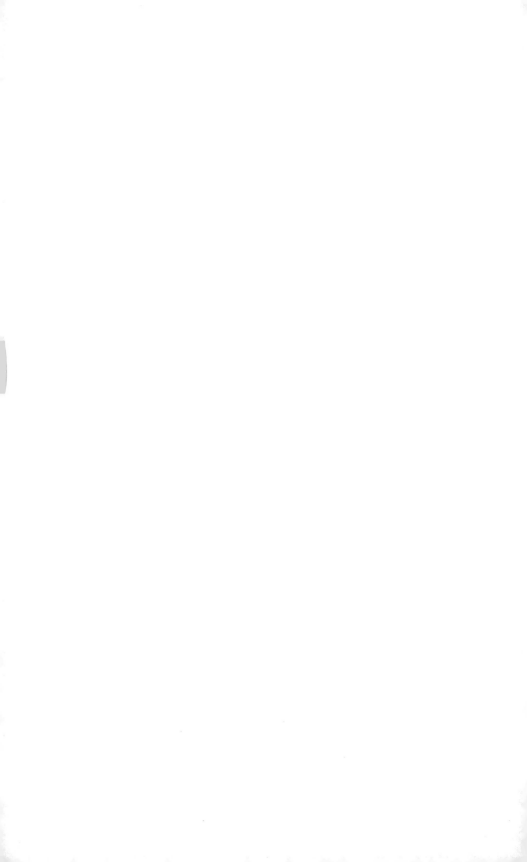

Lightning Source UK Ltd.
Milton Keynes UK
UKHW010000210722
406167UK00001B/264

9 781487 592141